D1483082

Trailing Clouds of Glory

Trailing Clouds of Glory

Spiritual Values in Children's Literature

by Madeleine L'Engle
with Avery Brooke, Anthologist

The Westminster Press
Philadelphia

Book design by Gene Harris

First edition

Published by The Westminster Press®
Philadelphia, Pennsylvania

PRINTED IN THE UNITED STATES OF AMERICA

9 8 7 6 5 4 3 2 1

Library of Congress Cataloging in Publication Data

L'Engle, Madeleine.
  Trailing clouds of glory.

  Includes indexes.
  1. Children's literature—History and criticism.
2. Religion in literature. I. Brooke, Avery. II. Title.
PN1009.A1L46 1985   809'.89282   84-29081
ISBN 0-664-32721-4

Acknowledgments

  The author and the anthologist gratefully acknowledge permission to use copyrighted material by the following:

Judy Blume: Reprinted with permission of Bradbury Press, Inc., from *It's Not the End of the World* by Judy Blume. Copyright © 1972 by Judy Blume.
Malcolm J. Bosse: Abridged from pp. 55–61 in *The 79 Squares* by Malcolm J. Bosse (Thomas Y. Crowell Co.). Copyright © 1979 by Malcolm J. Bosse. Reprinted by permission of Harper & Row, Publishers, Inc.
Ray Bradbury: Reprinted by permission of Don Congdon Associates, Inc., from *The Halloween Tree* by Ray Bradbury. Copyright © 1972 by Ray Bradbury.
Mary Ellen Chase: Reprinted with permission of Macmillan Publishing Company from *Windswept* by Mary Ellen Chase. Copyright 1941 and 1964 by Mary Ellen Chase.

Used by permission of The Canadian Publishers, McClelland and Stewart Limited, Toronto.

Katherine Paterson: From pp. 38–40 in *Bridge to Terabithia* by Katherine Paterson (Thomas Y. Crowell Co.). Copyright © 1977 by Katherine Paterson. Reprinted by permission of Harper & Row, Publishers, Inc.

Chaim Potok: From *In the Beginning* by Chaim Potok. Copyright © 1975 by Chaim Potok and Adena Potok, Trustee. Reprinted by permission of Alfred A. Knopf, Inc.

Barbara Robinson: Abridged from pp. 40–46 in *The Best Christmas Pageant Ever* by Barbara Robinson. Copyright © 1972 by Barbara Robinson. Reprinted by permission of Harper & Row, Publishers, Inc.

Colby Rodowsky: From *What About Me?* by Colby Rodowsky. Copyright © 1976 by Colby Rodowsky. Used by permission of Franklin Watts, Inc.

Antoine de Saint-Exupéry: Excerpt from *The Little Prince* by Antoine de Saint-Exupéry. Copyright 1943, 1971 by Harcourt Brace Jovanovich, Inc. Reprinted by permission of the publisher.

William Steig: Excerpts from *Abel's Island* by William Steig. Copyright © 1976 by William Steig. Reprinted by permission of Farrar, Straus and Giroux, Inc.

Noel Streatfeild: "Pauline Learns a Lesson" from *Ballet Shoes* by Noel Streatfeild. Copyright 1936 and renewed 1964 by Noel Streatfeild. Reprinted by permission of Alfred A. Knopf, Inc.

Hugh Walpole: Excerpts from *Jeremy* by Hugh Walpole. Reprinted by permission of Rupert Hart-Davis.

E. B. White: From pp. 175–181 in *Charlotte's Web* by E. B. White. Text copyright 1952, 1980 by E. B. White. Reprinted by permission of Harper & Row, Publishers, Inc.

T. H. White: Reprinted by permission of G. P. Putnam's Sons from *The Once and Future King* by T. H. White. Copyright 1939, 1940, by T. H. White, © 1958 by T. H. White.

Aaron Zeitlin: Selection from *If You Look at the Stars and Yawn* by Aaron Zeitlin, translated by Emanuel Goldsmith. Reprinted with permission of the B'nai B'rith Commission on Adult Jewish Education.

We also acknowledge and thank the many friends who helped us in collecting and choosing material for this book. We are especially grateful to Joy Chapman, for her help in research and for her enthusiastic support, and to the staff of the Darien Library, Darien, Connecticut, and in particular to Genevieve Betts, Ann Carnahan, Mary Freedman and Tina Reich. We also wish to thank the staffs of Middlesex Middle School Library in Darien and the Ferguson Library in Stamford, Connecticut.

Not in entire forgetfulness,
And not in utter nakedness,
But trailing clouds of glory do we come
From God, who is our home:
Heaven lies about us in our infancy!

William Wordsworth
"Intimations of Immortality"

Contents

Preface

A long time ago, when I was a very small child visiting my grandmother at her cottage on the beach, something happened after which nothing else could ever quite be the same. It must have been a glorious night for someone to have said, "Let's wake the baby and show her the stars."

My grandmother came into the room, untucked the mosquito netting, picked me up, and carried me out onto the beach. That was my first awareness of night, and my first vision of stars and of the Milky Way, trailing clouds of glory across the sky. And my first intuitive flash of knowledge that there is far more to everything than the dailiness of the everyday world. That first sight of the heavens stretched across the ocean and brilliant with stars was, although I was no way nearly old enough to call it that, my first numinous experience. And I will never look at the stars and yawn.

Adults may be weary with indifference, with noninvolvement, but no child is indifferent. Awareness of life and of the world around us is acute when we are children and, if we are blessed, will remain acute all our lives. Let us never stop asking questions, of ourselves, of each other, of God.

When I was a solitary only child growing up in New York City, I was, like all children, full of questions. And I found early, as soon as I could read easily by myself, that the best answers to my questions came not directly but through the stories I read. It was in story that I found hints of the meaning I sought: not fact, but meaning. Like everybody else moving out of very early childhood, I wanted to know what it's all about. Why are we born? Does my life make any difference? Does it matter? Does anybody care? Old, old questions. They've been around through the rise and fall of civilizations. But we all have to ask for ourselves.

Why do human beings make war? was another of my most

anguished questions. Why was my father (who was mustard-gassed in that war to end war) slowly and agonizingly coughing his lungs out? Why are nations still lining up against nations, and often in the name of religion?

Why did my heart ache with beauty when I saw a little sliver of a new moon above the building on the far side of the courtyard, as I stood looking out my bedroom window? Who were they, the young man and woman on the roof of the apartment building on my left? They were holding each other tightly and kissing as though afraid of being torn apart. What was their story? Whose voices were those I heard, laughing uproariously with the joy of being? Whose sobbing was it that I heard, coming from somewhere else in the echoing courtyard? What was this incredible business of life all about?

I turned to my bookcase and pulled out *Emily of New Moon*. Emily Byrd Starr was my friend and companion, closer to me than any of my classmates at school. She too was a solitary only child. Her father, too, was dying. She too had names for things, and wrote poetry, and was an awkward child. She too had the intuitive "flash" which helped affirm her being, sometimes in the darkest moments. She too wanted to be a writer.

There, in that bookcase, were many other friends: Toad of Toad Hall, with his overblown sense of importance that was so easily deflated; Heidi, who grew sick with homesickness away from her beloved snow-capped mountains; the Mad Hatter, who knew that time is not "it," but "he," and that if we quarrel with time he won't do anything we ask. There was Joseph, with his coat of many colors and his foolish bragging; the selfish giant whose garden was always gripped by winter's snow; Kay, with the splinter of ice deep in his heart. . . .

Last summer I walked with Avery Brooke the length of a wall of bookshelves, that original bookcase having long been outgrown, and said, "Oh, we must use this, and this, and this! We can't leave this one out! Oh, and here. . . ."

But in a brief anthology such as this, much has to be left out, for this collection doesn't pretend to be comprehensive. Being limited to a certain number of pages is good discipline; it also means deleting stories dear to our hearts. Avery spent long hours going through vast quantities of material, and the final selection is hers. Each one she has chosen says something special to me, and I hope will speak to the readers of this volume too.

Books written for children are usually affirmative; no one looks at the stars and yawns; there is passionate concern for the broken, the lost, the hurt. All my life through stories, those I read, and those I write, I have been building (intuitively, rather than consciously) a theology. The term "theology" means the word about God. So this anthology might well be called an expression of a theology, for the word about God can be built up of many simple things; it doesn't need to be pompous or pretentious; it is a way of looking at life and asking questions and finding stories.

Perhaps we may be asked why we are looking for a theology in children's books rather than in learned volumes of theology.

And the answer is a story:

Once there was a very wise rabbi. A young student came to see him and said, "Rabbi, in the old days, there were those who saw God. Why doesn't anybody see God nowadays?"

And the rabbi replied, "Oh, my child, nowadays nobody can stoop so low."

I'm nobody! Who are you?
Are you nobody, too?
Then there's a pair of us—don't tell!
They'd banish us, you know.

How dreary to be somebody!
How public, like a frog
To tell your name the livelong June
To an admiring bog!

Emily Dickinson

1
I'm Nobody!
Who Are You?

It took my father until I was nearly eighteen to finish coughing out his lungs. In *Emily of New Moon* by Lucy M. Montgomery, Emily's father was killed more quickly and mercifully by tuberculosis. Her mother was long dead. She was going to be very much alone, torn from every place she knew, everybody she loved. And in the midst of this grief came "the flash."

What was "the flash"? I suspect that all of us who have known it, one way or another, would describe it differently, for it is unique to each person in the way in which it is received, though the source, I believe, is the same.

She loved the spruce barrens, away at the further end of the long, sloping pasture. That was a place where magic was made. She came more fully into her fairy birthright there than in any other place. Nobody who saw Emily skimming over the bare field would have envied her. She was little and pale and poorly clad; sometimes she shivered in her thin jacket; yet a queen might have gladly given a crown for her visions—her dreams of wonder. . . .

And then, for one glorious, supreme moment, came "the flash."

Emily called it that, although she felt that the name didn't exactly describe it. It couldn't be described—not even to Father, who always seemed a little puzzled by it. Emily never spoke of it to any one else.

It had always seemed to Emily, ever since she could remember, that she was very, very near to a world of wonderful beauty. Between it and herself hung only a thin curtain; she could never draw the curtain aside—but sometimes, just for a moment, a wind fluttered it and then it was as if she caught a glimpse of the enchanting realm beyond—only a glimpse—and heard a note of unearthly music.

This moment came rarely—went swiftly, leaving her breathless with the inexpressible delight of it. She could never recall it—never summon it—never pretend it; but the wonder of it stayed with her for days. It never came twice with the same thing. To-night the dark boughs against that far-off sky had given it. It had come with a high, wild note of wind in the night, with a shadow wave over a ripe field, with a greybird lighting on her window-sill in a storm, with the singing of "Holy, holy, holy" in church, with a glimpse of the kitchen fire when she had come home on a dark autumn night, with the spirit-like blue of ice palms on a twilit pane, with a felicitous new word when she was writing down a "description" of something. And always when the flash came to her Emily felt that life was a wonderful, mysterious thing of persistent beauty.

When Emily's father was dying, he told her:

"We'll stay together to the very end, then, little Emily-child. We won't be parted for a minute. And I want you to be brave. You mustn't be afraid of *anything,* Emily. Death isn't terrible. The universe is full of love—and spring comes everywhere—and in death you open and shut a door. There are beautiful things on the other side of the door. I'll find your mother there—I've doubted many things, but I've never doubted *that.* Sometimes I've been afraid that she would get so far ahead of me in the ways of eternity that I'd never catch up. But I feel *now* that she's waiting for me. And we'll wait for you—we won't hurry—we'll loiter and linger till you catch up with us."

"I wish you—could take me right through the door with you," whispered Emily.

"After a little while you won't wish that. You have yet to learn how kind time is. And life has something for you—I feel it. Go forward to meet it fearlessly, dear. I know you don't feel like that just now—but you will remember my words by and by."

"I feel just now," said Emily, who couldn't bear to hide anything from Father, "that I don't like God any more."

Douglas Starr laughed—the laugh Emily liked best. It was such a dear laugh—she caught her breath over the dearness of it. She felt his arms tightening round her.

"Yes, you do, honey. You can't help liking God. He is Love itself, you know. You mustn't mix Him up with Ellen Greene's God, of course."

Emily didn't know exactly what Father meant. But all at once she found that she wasn't afraid any longer—and the bitterness had gone out of her sorrow, and the unbearable pain out of her heart. She felt as if love was all about her and around her, breathed out from some great, invisible, hovering Tenderness. One couldn't be afraid or bitter where love was—and love was everywhere. Father was going through the door—no, he was going to lift a curtain—she liked *that* thought better, because a curtain wasn't as hard and fast as a door— and he would slip into that world of which the flash had given her glimpses. He would be there in its beauty—never very far away from her. She could bear anything if she could only feel that Father wasn't very far away from her—just beyond that wavering curtain.

In telling Emily not to confuse God with Ellen Greene's God, Emily's father was giving her an extremely important warning. Montaigne wrote, "Oh, senseless man who cannot make a worm, and yet makes gods by dozens."

Ellen Greene's God was not "Love itself," as Emily's father affirmed. Ellen Greene could see terrible, unjust things happen and say smugly, "It's God's will." Ellen Greene reminds me of the woman who kept berating her husband for his past faults, and when he begged her to stop, saying that he thought she had "forgiven and forgotten," she replied, "Of course I have forgiven and forgotten. I just don't want you ever to forget that I've forgiven and forgotten."

Because Emily's father taught her that God is Love itself, and because she had learned about grief and death while she was still a child, she was also given a strong sense of her own self, not an individualistic sense of self, apart from the rest of the universe, but a self that is part of all creation.

It's only those who set themselves, as selves, apart from others, who are like the frog in Emily Dickinson's poem. And of course there are many other frogs in many other stories who are different, frogs who were once princes and who are waiting for the kiss that will release them from the wicked spell.

In one fairy tale a frog finds the princess's golden ball in his pond. She begs him to give it back to her, "and I'll do anything you say." The frog retrieves the ball and gives it to her, on the condition that he sit by her at the table and eat from her plate.

The princess takes the ball, but then she doesn't want to fulfill her part of the bargain. She is horrified at having a slimy frog sit by her and take food from her fork.

The king, her father, is displeased with her indeed. He has taught her that a princess is always courteous and honors her promises.

The princess, who has, after all, been well trained, lets the frog sit on the table by her plate and, hiding her revulsion, with gracious courtesy, feeds the frog from her fork.

And of course he stops being a frog and becomes a prince.

The rednecks in Harper Lee's *To Kill a Mockingbird* may not turn into princes, but their response to the open and innocent courtesy of Scout is almost as marvelous.

It was not so long ago that segregation was taken for granted in most parts of this country, not only in the South. Far worse than segregation itself was lynching, a horror that lingered in the South long after such an action became intolerable to men of reason, like Scout's lawyer father, Atticus. It is difficult to understand how men who went to church with their wives on Sunday, sang the hymns, and said the prayers could see taking the law into their own hands, and lynching a man, as being part of God's purpose. But it is good to think of Atticus. Since I'm half Southern, I've had the privilege of knowing a number of such thoughtful and compassionate lawyers.

Atticus gave his children, Scout and Jem, the same kind of training in courtesy and honor that the king in the fairy tale gave the princess. It is Scout's open good manners that stop the lynching, as much as Atticus's determination. It was a goodly heritage that Atticus gave Scout and Jem.

I dressed quickly. We waited until Aunty's light went out, and we walked quietly down the back steps. There was no moon tonight. . . .

Atticus's office was in the courthouse when he began his law practice, but after several years of it he moved to quieter quarters in the Maycomb Bank building. When we rounded the corner of the square, we saw the car parked in front of the bank. "He's in there," said Jem.

But he wasn't. His office was reached by a long hallway. Looking down the hall, we should have seen *Atticus Finch, Attorney-at-Law* in small sober letters against the light from behind his door. It was dark.

Jem peered in the bank door to make sure. He turned the knob. The door was locked. "Let's go up the street. Maybe he's visitin' Mr. Underwood."

Mr. Underwood not only ran *The Maycomb Tribune* office, he lived in it. That is, above it. He covered the courthouse and jailhouse news simply by looking out his upstairs window. The office building was on the northwest corner of the square, and to reach it we had to pass the jail. . . . The jail was Maycomb's only conversation piece: its detractors said it looked like a Victorian privy; its supporters said it gave the town a good solid respectable look, and no stranger would ever suspect that it was full of niggers.

As we walked up the sidewalk, we saw a solitary light burning in the distance. "That's funny," said Jem, "jail doesn't have an outside light."

"Looks like it's over the door," said Dill.

A long extension cord ran between the bars of a second-floor window and down the side of the building. In the light from its bare bulb, Atticus was sitting propped against the front door. He was sitting in one of his office chairs, and he was reading, oblivious of the nightbugs dancing over his head.

I made to run, but Jem caught me. "Don't go to him," he said, "he might not like it. He's all right, let's go home. I just wanted to see where he was."

We were taking a short cut across the square when four dusty cars came in from the Meridian highway, moving slowly in a line. They went around the square, passed the bank building, and stopped in front of the jail.

Nobody got out. We saw Atticus look up from his newspaper. He closed it, folded it deliberately, dropped it in his lap, and pushed his hat to the back of his head. He seemed to be expecting them.

"Come on," whispered Jem. We streaked across the square, across the street, until we were in the shelter of the Jitney Jungle door. Jem peeked up the sidewalk. "We can get closer," he said. We ran to Tyndal's Hardware door—near enough, at the same time discreet.

In ones and twos, men got out of the cars. Shadows became substance as light revealed solid shapes moving toward the jail door. Atticus remained where he was. The men hid him from view.

"He in there, Mr. Finch?" a man said.

"He is," we heard Atticus answer, "and he's asleep. Don't wake him up."

In obedience to my father, there followed what I later realized was a sickeningly comic aspect of an unfunny situation: the men talked in near-whispers.

"You know what we want," another man said. "Get aside from the door, Mr. Finch."

"You can turn around and go home again, Walter," Atticus said pleasantly. "Heck Tate's around somewhere."

"The hell he is," said another man. "Heck's bunch's so deep in the woods they won't get out til mornin'."

"Indeed? Why so?"

"Called 'em off on a snipe hunt," was the succinct answer. "Didn't you think a'that, Mr. Finch?"

"Thought about it, but didn't believe it. Well then," my father's voice was still the same, "that changes things, doesn't it?"

"It do," another deep voice said. Its owner was a shadow.

"Do you really think so?"

This was the second time I heard Atticus ask that question in two days, and it meant somebody's man would get jumped. This was too good to miss. I broke away from Jem and ran as fast as I could to Atticus.

Jem shrieked and tried to catch me, but I had a lead on him and Dill. I pushed my way through dark smelly bodies and burst into the circle of light.

"H-ey, Atticus!"

I thought he would have a fine surprise, but his face killed my joy. A flash of plain fear was going out of his eyes, but returned when Dill and Jem wriggled into the light.

There was a smell of stale whiskey and pigpen about, and when I glanced around I discovered that these men were strangers. They were not the people I saw last night. Hot embarrassment shot through me: I had leaped triumphantly into a ring of people I had never seen before.

Atticus got up from his chair, but he was moving slowly, like an old man. He put the newspaper down very carefully, adjusting its creases with lingering fingers. They were trembling a little.

"Go home, Jem," he said. "Take Scout and Dill home."

We were accustomed to prompt, if not always cheerful acquiescence to Atticus's instructions, but from the way he stood Jem was not thinking of budging.

"Go home, I said."

Jem shook his head. As Atticus's fists went to his hips, so did Jem's, and as they faced each other I could see little resemblance between them: Jem's soft brown hair and eyes, his oval face and snug-fitting ears were our mother's, contrasting oddly with Atticus's graying black hair and square-cut features, but they were somehow alike. Mutual defiance made them alike.

"Son, I said go home."

Jem shook his head.

"I'll send him home," a burly man said, and grabbed Jem roughly by the collar. He yanked Jem nearly off his feet.

"Don't you touch him!" I kicked the man swiftly. Barefooted, I was surprised to see him fall back in real pain. I intended to kick his shin, but aimed too high.

"That'll do, Scout." Atticus put his hand on my shoulder. "Don't kick folks. No—" he said, as I was pleading justification.

"Ain't nobody gonna do Jem that way," I said.

"All right, Mr. Finch, get 'em outa here," someone growled. "You got fifteen seconds to get 'em outa here."

In the midst of this strange assembly, Atticus stood trying to make Jem mind him. "I ain't going," was his steady answer to Atticus's threats, requests, and finally, "Please, Jem, take them home."

I was getting a bit tired of that, but felt Jem had his own reasons for doing as he did, in view of his prospects once Atticus did get him home. I looked around the crowd. It was a summer's night, but the men were dressed, most of them, in overalls and denim shirts buttoned up to the collars. I thought they must be cold-natured, as their sleeves were unrolled and buttoned at the cuffs. Some wore hats pulled firmly down over their ears. They were sullen-looking, sleepy-eyed men who seemed unused to late hours. I sought once more for a familiar face, and at the center of the semi-circle I found one.

"Hey, Mr. Cunningham."

The man did not hear me, it seemed.

"Hey, Mr. Cunningham. How's your entailment gettin' along?"

Mr. Walter Cunningham's legal affairs were well known to me; Atticus had once described them at length. The big man blinked and hooked his thumbs in his overall straps. He seemed uncomfortable; he cleared his throat and looked away. My friendly overture had fallen flat.

Mr. Cunningham wore no hat, and the top half of his forehead was white in contrast to his sunscorched face, which led me to believe that he wore one most days. He shifted his feet, clad in heavy work shoes.

"Don't you remember me, Mr. Cunningham? I'm Jean Louise Finch. You brought us some hickory nuts one time, remember?" I began to sense the futility one feels when unacknowledged by a chance acquaintance.

"I go to school with Walter," I began again. "He's your boy, ain't he? Ain't he, sir?"

Mr. Cunningham was moved to a faint nod. He did know me, after all.

"He's in my grade," I said, "and he does right well. He's a good boy," I added, "a real nice boy. We brought him home for dinner one time. Maybe he told you about me, I beat him up one time but he was real nice about it. Tell him hey for me, won't you?"

Atticus had said it was the polite thing to talk to people about what they were interested in, not about what you were interested in. Mr.

Cunningham displayed no interest in his son, so I tackled his entailment once more in a last-ditch effort to make him feel at home.

"Entailments are bad," I was advising him, when I slowly awoke to the fact that I was addressing the entire aggregation. The men were all looking at me, some had their mouths half-open. Atticus had stopped poking at Jem: they were standing together beside Dill. Their attention amounted to fascination. Atticus's mouth, even, was half-open, an attitude he had once described as uncouth. Our eyes met and he shut it.

"Well, Atticus, I was just sayin' to Mr. Cunningham that entailments are bad an' all that, but you said not to worry, it takes a long time sometimes . . . that you all'd ride it out together . . ." I was slowly drying up, wondering what idiocy I had committed. Entailments seemed all right enough for livingroom talk.

I began to feel sweat gathering at the edges of my hair; I could stand anything but a bunch of people looking at me. They were quite still.

"What's the matter?" I asked.

Atticus said nothing. I looked around and up at Mr. Cunningham, whose face was equally impassive. Then he did a peculiar thing. He squatted down and took me by both shoulders.

"I'll tell him you said hey, little lady," he said.

Then he straightened up and waved a big paw. "Let's clear out," he called. "Let's get going, boys."

As they had come, in ones and twos the men shuffled back to their ramshackle cars. Doors slammed, engines coughed, and they were gone.

I turned to Atticus, but Atticus had gone to the jail and was leaning against it with his face to the wall. I went to him and pulled his sleeve. "Can we go home now?" He nodded, produced his handkerchief, gave his face a going-over and blew his nose violently.

"Mr. Finch?" A soft husky voice came from the darkness above: "They gone?"

Atticus stepped back and looked up. "They've gone," he said. "Get some sleep, Tom. They won't bother you any more."

Scout and Jem are who they are because their father is who he is. We do not become who we are in isolation; becoming human is something that happens in community, whatever community we happen to be in. In *What About Me?* Colby Rodowsky emphasizes this growing into who we are through interrelationship. Dorrie is Dorrie within the circle of her family, and Dorrie's family includes her brother, Fredlet, who has Down's syndrome. Fredlet is never going to be able to grow up to be a normal human being, and Fredlet's problems are not just his own but the problems of the family, his parents, his sister.

Dorrie has to learn some of the most difficult lessons of love: She can hate Fredlet even while she loves him. She can run away from him physically, but she cannot run away from the *fact* of Fredlet. Fredlet *is*, and that is going to make Dorrie a different human being from what she would be if Fredlet were normal, or if he had never been born at all.

In this time where the pursuit of pleasure and the avoidance of pain are heralded as the greatest good, Dorrie's lessons of love are hard fought. But had Fredlet been kept away from Dorrie in order to spare her, she would not have been given the opportunities for strength she was given. Fredlet, one might say, was a kind of fairy-tale frog, though there is no way he can be kissed into the handsome prince. But that, too, is part of the story.

Still, I wonder. About me, and Fredlet, and Mom and Dad, and Guntzie, and the spring of my sophomore year in high school. But mostly I wonder about Fredlet.

Fredlet: my brother and that spring when I was fifteen he was eleven—except in his head he was more like three.

And I hated him.

Honest-to-God hate. Not all the time; not every day; but enough to scare me sometimes. But then other times I wanted to sit down next to him on the floor and listen to that blasted *Sesame Street* record with him, and let him show me stuff out of the Sears, Roebuck catalog; it was a 1964 catalog, but not to Fredlet. If that's not the kind of thing to make you want to throw the psych book in the incinerator and switch to typing, I don't know what is.

It had always been a sort of love-hate thing with me and Fredlet, ever since the day my mother brought him home from the hospital. I remember, because I was four and had on new Sunday shoes and I wasn't sure whether I felt all excited because of the new shoes or the baby or because my mother was coming home. I remember that my mother wasn't fat anymore and I could get my arms all the way around her waist. Mom sat down on the couch and Dad put the blue blanket thing in her arms and she said, "Look, Dorrie. Here he is. Your very own brother, Freddie."

And right then I said it. "Piglet. He looks like Piglet, Momma." It had been my sort of Winnie the Pooh period (you know, the way Picasso had his blue period), and I thought why couldn't we have a

Pooh Bear baby, or even a Roo. "No, Momma. He's Piglet, Piglet, Piglet." And I stamped my foot and the new Sunday shoe sounded like a slap on the hard wood floor. Somehow I must have gotten the feeling that my mother was upset because I remember reaching out and touching the baby's cheek. "Okay, Momma. He's Fredlet, then, Poor Fredlet." And his cheek felt cool as marble.

Looking back, I guess it was his eyes that told me what I didn't know I knew, or what nobody else had even dared to think. It was always his eyes, and his tongue, and later on a lot of other things, or rather not doing a lot of other things that led to the doctors and the tests and the answers we didn't want to hear.

The word *mongoloid.*

My mother still can't say that word without her voice catching. *Mongoloid. Mongoloid.* And the school for retarded children, except that they call them exceptional children. I never really understood that. Like maybe the parents didn't know which end of "exceptional" they had.

Mom and Dad always called him Fred, but to almost everybody else—and especially to me—Fredlet never got over being Fredlet. . . .

I shook some cornflakes into a bowl and pulled my chair up to the table, concentrating on the back of the cereal box. Dad stood up.

"I've got to run now, Dorrie. I have a brief to get ready."

"Where are you going?" asked my mother, coming into the kitchen. "Did you forget we have to take Fred to the dentist?"

"Oh, good lord, is that today? I've got to get to the office. This brief is due Monday."

"But you promised. You know what Fred's like at the dentist. I purposely made the appointment for a Saturday because you said you'd come with us."

"I'm sorry, Elizabeth. I really am. But I have a full day's work. That court case last week ran over and I'm a day behind."

"Never mind," said Mom, pouring herself a cup of coffee. But her tone of voice said much more. Like:

"I'll manage, but it won't be easy—"

"After all, you said you'd help—"

"You could go to the office this afternoon—"

"Or tomorrow."

"I'm sure you can manage," said Dad. "It's just for a checkup. I'm going to run now. I'll be in the office if you need me."

Mom sighed. "I guess we'll manage," she said as she left the room. She didn't stomp, but I had the feeling if Mom had been a stomper she would have stomped that morning—or slammed, or yelled. Mom was a teeth-clencher instead.

"Uh, Dorrie," said Dad from the kitchen door, "how about it? Want to do me a favor?"

"Okay. I guess so. What is it?" But I knew, without really having to ask. Fredlet, again—and again and again.

"How about going along with your mother? You know how Fred is about dentists. You'll be home by noon."

"Sure. Okay. It's okay." To me my words sounded dull and heavy.

"That's great. I'll tell your mother. Fred is sometimes a lot for her to handle alone. Thanks."

I sat in the empty kitchen looking down at the bowl of soggy cornflakes. It wasn't exactly that I minded so much having to go with Mom and Fredlet. It was more that nobody especially cared whether or not I had anything else to do. I mean, anything to do as me— Dorrie Shafer—like a drawing that just had to be done or a hunk of clay I was just aching to get my fingers around. "What are *you* doing today, Dorrie? What do you think about? What do you feel?" Instead of fredletfredletfredletfredletfredletfredletfredletfredlet. . . .

We could have taken a taxi. That would have been so simple. Two empty cabs even slowed down to see if we were interested, but all the time Fredlet kept saying, "Bus—go bus. Fredlet go vrrmm." So we waited for the bus.

While my mother paid the fare I settled Fredlet on the long seat behind the driver. And right away he started turning his imaginary steering wheel.

"Vrrmm, vrrmm, vrrmm," he roared as the bus bounced down Lexington Avenue. "Vrrmm, vrrmm." He twisted that wheel right and left. "Vrrmm, screeeech, whoa," he shouted every time the bus slowed down.

Farther back by the center door there was a bunch of boys hooting and calling out, "That's right, kid. You get us there. Vrrmm, vrrmm." My face burned. I looked over at my mother, but she was staring out the windows on the other side. Staring out as hard as she could.

All of a sudden something bounced off Fredlet's head and rolled down the front of him. "Come along, Fred. We're almost ready to get off," said Mom, tugging at his sleeve, but Fredlet shook her off and bent down to get the scrunched-up paper cup. For a minute he held it gently in his hand as if it were—oh, I don't know—maybe a butterfly. Then he grabbed my hand and pulled me back toward the laughing boys.

"Here—here—here's your paper and how-do-you-do-today," said Fredlet, bowing to the boys. He put his hand out to the biggest boy and said, "How do *you* do today?" and the way he said it you just knew that Fredlet wanted to know. Really. The boy looked funny, then he looked at his friends, then he blushed. Then he shook Fredlet's hand.

"Come on, Fredlet. We're going to miss our stop." I got him off that bus, somehow. And for a moment I thought maybe I was going to cry—right there in the middle of Lexington Avenue.

"Oh, Mom," I said, "he talks to everyone. Someday he's going to get hurt."

My mother caught hold of Fredlet's arm. "He's friendly. Don't take that away from him. When I walk him to school every day there are people all along the way who speak to him, and know him by name."

All of a sudden it occurred to me that I'd never thought very much about what Mom and Fredlet did all day. I knew Fredlet went to a special school in a converted brownstone on Eighty-third Street. I'd even been there for programs and all. But I never thought about it being an everyday thing.

Fredlet really didn't seem to care where we were going till we opened the door of Dr. Jason's waiting room. I guess it was the smell that told him. "Oooh—oooh—oooh," he moaned, clapping his hand on his jaw. "Oooh—oooh," and he shuffled across the waiting room and curled up in a large chair. He put his head down under his arm like some giant wailing bird.

I sat as far away from him as I could and hid my face behind a *Time* magazine. "Maybe nobody will know I'm with him," I hoped, trying to tune out his moaning. Wouldn't you know it, but some old busybody started in. "Oh, the poor thing. Does he have a tooth-ache?" My mother answered her, but I wouldn't have bothered.

"No, not really. It's time for a checkup and he doesn't like dentists much. But Dr. Jason's very good with him."

"Oh, the poor little thing," the old hag babbled on. "How old is he?"

I clutched the magazine as hard as I could. "Oh, why doesn't she shut up?" I thought. "He's not a little thing, and it's none of her business how he is. Oh, why does Mom even talk to her?"

Just then the nurse spoke to my mother. "Mrs. Shafer, we're ready for Fred now." Mom got this what-do-we-do-now look on her face. "Come on, Dorrie. Let's see if we can get him to go in," she said to me in a voice that said point-blank, "You know we can't." Mom stood beside Fredlet. "Come along, Fred. It's your turn now. Let's go see Dr. Jason." Fredlet never stopped his wailing. He never took his head out from under his arm. "Please, Fred, show Dorrie what a good boy you are. When you're all finished, we'll have ice cream."

"You try," she said, stepping back. Suddenly I felt as if a hundred eyes were boring into my back. I tried to pull Fredlet's arm away from his head, but he just burrowed deeper into the chair.

"Fredlet. Please, Fredlet. For me, Dorrie."

Just then Dr. Jason came up behind me. "Need any help here?" he asked. As soon as Fredlet heard his voice he shut up. "Okay, Fred. Let's go," said Dr. Jason, taking hold of Fredlet's arm. "Come along. I have a lot to show you in my office, and I want to clean those teeth."

Fredlet stumbled to his feet. His face was streaked with real tears, and for some reason I was surprised. Dr. Jason swooped Fredlet away and waved Mom and me back onto the couch all in one gesture.

I buried my face back in *Time* magazine, hoping my mother wouldn't talk to me. But she did. "It's funny, but he's always better for someone else." I bit my lip to keep from saying what I thought. "You're his mother. You ought to be able to handle him." I read the same words over and over.

"Aaw—help—Maa." All of a sudden the god-awful screams tore through the office. I could feel my mother stiffening on the couch next to me, but I wouldn't look at her. "Aaach—no—no."

The nurse stuck her nose out into the waiting room. "Don't worry, Mrs. Shafer. The doctor's really not hurting him at all."

"Oh, I'm sure he's not, but shouldn't I go back there with him?"

"Oh, no," hurried the nurse. "We can manage Fred better alone, I think." And she pulled her head back into the office, this time closing the door.

The chokes and screams reached through that closed door like giant fingers closing around me. And in the background I kept hearing my mother's inane conversation with that stupid woman. "Oh, I'm sure he's all right. It's just hard for him to understand."

All of a sudden I felt encased in ice. I wasn't sure whether my feet or hands would move. My throat felt frozen. I knew I had to get out of that waiting room. I couldn't stand it another minute.

And I ran. I threw the magazine on the table and I ran.

Dorrie named her retarded brother Fredlet. Had he been normal, the "let" would have been dropped as he grew older. What we are named by others and by ourselves does influence *who* we are. If a girl named Philippa is called *Pill* by her classmates, that isn't going to help her to become open and loving. Somehow, the hurtful nickname has to be changed.

A teacher I loved and admired once said to me, when I was being particularly stupid about an algebra problem, "Honestly, Madeleine. Honestly, Maddening," but she said it with such affection that we laughed, and I was able to understand the problem a little better.

When I was twelve years old, and in an English boarding school, we were all numbered. I was Number 97, and I think that this being numbered, rather than being called by name, began intuitively, my intense concern about Naming and being Named.

In my book *A Wind in the Door*, Meg says:

"No, I'm much too excited to be hungry, but if I don't turn up on time, it won't go down very well if I explain that I was late because I was talking with a cherubim. My mother doesn't like tardiness, either."

Proginoskes said, "Much can be accomplished in an hour. We have to find out what our first ordeal is."

"Don't you know?"

"Why would I know?"

"You're a cherubim."

"Even a cherubim has limits. When three ordeals are planned, then nobody knows ahead of time what they are; even the Teacher may not know."

"Then what do we do? How do we find out?"

Proginoskes waved several wings slowly back and forth in thought, which would have felt very pleasant on a hot day, but which, on a cold morning, made Meg turn up the collar of her jacket. The cherubim did not notice; he continued waving and thinking. Then she could feel his words moving slowly, tentatively, within her mind. "If you've been assigned to me, I suppose you must be some kind of a Namer, too, even if a primitive one."

"A what?"

"A Namer. For instance, the last time I was with a Teacher—or at school, as you call it—my assignment was to memorize the names of the stars."

"Which stars?"

"All of them."

"You mean *all* the stars, in *all* the galaxies?"

"Yes, If he calls for one of them, someone has to know which one he means. Anyhow, they like it; there aren't many who know them all by name, and if your name isn't known, then it's a very lonely feeling."

"Am I supposed to learn the names of all the stars, too?" It was an appalling thought.

"Good galaxy, no!"

"Then what *am* I supposed to do?"

Proginoskes waved several wings, which, Meg was learning, was more or less his way of expressing "I haven't the faintest idea."

"Well, then, if I'm a Namer, what does that mean? What does a Namer do?"

The wings drew together, the eyes closed, singly, and in groups, until all were shut. Small puffs of mist-like smoke rose, swirled about him. "When I was memorizing the names of the stars, part of the purpose was to help them each to be more particularly the particular star each one was supposed to be. That's basically a Namer's job. Maybe you're supposed to make earthlings feel more human."

"What's that supposed to mean?" She sat down on the rock beside him; she was somehow no longer afraid of his wildness, his size, his spurts of fire.

He asked, "How do I make you feel?"

She hesitated, not wanting to be rude, forgetting that the cherubim, far more than Charles Wallace, did not need her outward words to know what was being said within. But she answered truthfully, "Confused."

Several puffs of smoke went up. "Well, we don't know each other very well yet. Who makes you least confused?"

"Calvin." There was no hesitation here. "When I'm with Calvin, I don't mind being me."

"You mean he makes you *more* you, don't you?"

"I guess you could put it that way."

"Who makes you feel the least you?"

"Mr. Jenkins . . . I was always getting sent to his office. He never understands anything, and everything I do is automatically wrong."

Sometimes we name things in our hearts, without being able to pronounce the word with our lips. When Marco is rescued from prison in Frances Hodgson Burnett's *The Lost Prince*, his friend, known as "The Rat," couldn't understand.

"Did you shout?" The Rat asked. "I didn't know you shouted."

"I didn't. I said nothing aloud. But I—the myself that is in me," Marco touched himself on his breast, "called out, 'Help! Help!' with all its strength. And help came."

The Rat regarded him dubiously.

"What did it call to?" he asked.

"To the Power—to the Strength-place—to the Thought that does things. The Buddhist hermit, who told my father about it, called it 'The Thought that thought the World.' "

A reluctant suspicion betrayed itself in The Rat's eyes.

"Do you mean you prayed?" he inquired, with a slight touch of disfavor.

Marco's eyes remained fixed upon him in vague thoughtfulness for a moment or so of pause.

"I don't know," he said at last. "Perhaps it's the same thing—when you need something so much that you cry out loud for it. But it's not words, it's a strong thing without a name."

We must be careful how we name. Jesus pointed out, forcefully, how wrong it is to call someone else stupid, or a fool.

My teacher could call me "Maddening" because she cared about me and was convinced that I was capable of mastering the algebra problem. Had she considered me stupid, she could have used the same words and they would have been destructive instead of constructive.

Penelope, in James Forman's *The Skies of Crete*, hears her grand-father calling her cousin Alexis a coward. Coward is an ugly word, a devastating word. The grandfather, Old Markos, is undoubtedly a brave man, a man who would never be called "coward." And yet Alexis not only faces him but dares to contradict him.

"Emmanuel," he said, "You've got my revolvers somewhere. Has Alexis seen them?"

"No!" said Alexis and Emmanuel more or less together, both with consternation.

"Well, let's have them out here on the table. It's time to talk of guns."

"Frankly, sir," said Alexis, "I'm not fond of guns."

"A grandson of mine? We'll soon change that. Get the guns, Emmanuel!" Emmanuel went reluctantly; Penelope knew he had long since buried the weapons at Katerina's insistence.

"So you don't like guns, eh? Do you love your country, boy? . . .

"You've a lifetime to sit still, boy, and hold your tongue. But now you're conversing with me, your grandfather. At least I'm speaking to you. Everyone loves his country. Everyone's patriotic."

"I'm nothing," said Alexis. "I only wish you would leave me alone." Penelope opened her eyes wide. She had never heard such a despairing voice. And what Old Markos might have said, no one would know, for Emmanuel entered with the guns, blackly tarnished, far from the bright destroyers Markos had pictured.

"Good Lord! My guns?" He picked them up, let the hammers fall. "Well, they still work and that's what matters." Shoving the guns across the table toward Alexis, he added, "It takes a good man to pull those triggers. Try it." Alexis refused to touch them. The evening was an ordeal for him.

"Let him be," said the shepherd. "Pick on me if you like."

Old Markos said, "I never pick on anyone smaller than myself and I'm not concerned with driving frightened puppies into battle. We need men with courage who love their country and are ready to fight. I'm speaking of Emmanuel. He's the one to organize the villagers." They looked at the old man, nonplused. "Naturally; who's more respected here?"

All this time Emmanuel had kept his own counsel, but now he would have to speak out. Penelope waited breathless, sure that he shared his father's defiant spirit, wondering only what words he would choose. Would he speak as a poet, the way he spoke of spring?

"Perhaps the time for that sort of fighting is over," said Emmanuel calmly.

"I only said 'perhaps,' " he cautioned, as Markos ground his teeth and Penelope stared. "Alexis, now, has been there. He's seen these new weapons. Men can only do so much with their bare hands. Perhaps it's all up to the great armies now."

"But Papa, are you saying we should run away?" said Penelope, her voice shrill with disbelief.

"I don't know what I'm saying," said Emmanuel. "Perhaps a man belongs in the army, not on his own. We'll have to wait and pray and when the time comes, make our own decisions."

"There's only one decision . . . *fight!* Look at this house; the best in town. You don't think you'll go on quietly farming, do you? They'll take everything if you permit them to and leave you beggars in the street."

Penelope knew Old Markos was right. There was no other answer.

"I'd rather be a beggar than kill a man," said Alexis.

"You!" said Old Markos, nothing more, but the single word bore all the venom of an inquisitor pronouncing sentence. Doggedly Alexis persisted; he would never fire a gun. What a queer cousin she had, thought Penelope. He was as conspicuous a coward as she had ever met, and yet he had the pluck to contradict Markos, a thing few men would dare.

Penelope had to learn that there are many kinds of cowardice and many kinds of bravery. Physical bravery is sometimes easier than standing up for what we believe. One has to be very brave to accept being called a coward because of conviction. Penelope had to ask herself who, ultimately, was the wiser, the braver, Old Markos or Alexis?

It was something the Quakers, the Society of Friends, had to think about. After he became a Quaker, William Penn asked George Fox if it was still all right for him to wear his sword on state occasions. And Fox replied, "Of course—if thee can."

Praise Me, says God;
I will know that you love Me.

Curse Me, says God;
I will know that you love Me.

Sing out My graces, says God.

Raise your fist against Me and revile.

Sing out My praises or revile.

Reviling is also a kind of praise, says God.

But if you sit fenced off
in your apathy, says God.

If you sit entrenched in:
"I don't give a hang."

If you look at the stars and yawn,

If you see suffering and don't cry out,

If you don't praise and don't revile,

Then I created you in vain, says God.

Aaron Zeitlin, translated by
Emanuel Goldsmith

2

If You Look
at the Stars and Yawn

Now there was a certain thief who used to pass the shrine of a god every day on his way to the market to pilfer. There wasn't a day that he did not fail to spit on the deity's shrine; some days he had to clear weeds or snow from the little shelter in order to take perfect aim. But this he did without exception, before he spat. On the day of the thief's death he was met by the god, who escorted him to the other life. The thief exclaimed in confusion, "Why are you doing me this honor? There was not a day when I didn't revile your shrine." The god answered, "That was more attention than my priests paid to me."

John, in his Revelation, says of the churches in Laodicea: "I know thy works, that thou art neither cold nor hot: I would thou wert cold or hot. So then because thou art lukewarm, and neither cold nor hot, I will spew thee out of my mouth."

The Herdmans, in Barbara Robinson's *The Best Christmas Pageant Ever,* were anything but lukewarm. They reviled more than they blessed, but they were not lukewarm. They were terrible kids. They pinched, kicked, swore, were noisy, had no respect for authority, infuriated everybody, including their father, who walked out, and their mother, who worked a double shift.

When, for the first time in their lives, they encountered the Christmas story, their response was not lukewarm. They reacted to hearing the story of Love itself with typical passion, blessing Mary, reviling Herod.

But they began to learn to bless as well as to revile, and the Christmas star did not make them yawn.

The thing was, the Herdmans didn't know anything about the Christmas story. They knew that Christmas was Jesus' birthday, but everything else was news to them—the shepherds, the Wise Men, the star, the stable, the crowded inn. . . .

"They never went to church in their whole life till your little brother told them we got refreshments," Alice said, "and all you ever hear about Christmas in school is how to make ornaments out of aluminum foil. So how would they know about the Christmas story?"

She was right. Of course they might have read about it, but they never read anything except "Amazing Comics." And they might have heard about it on TV, except that Ralph paid sixty-five cents for their TV at a garage sale, and you couldn't see anything on it unless somebody held on to the antenna. Even then, you couldn't see much.

The only other way for them to hear about the Christmas story was from their parents, and I guess Mr. Herdman never got around to it before he climbed on the railroad train. And it was pretty clear that Mrs. Herdman had given up ever trying to tell them anything.

So they just didn't know. And Mother said she had better begin by reading the Christmas story from the Bible. This was a pain in the neck to most of us because we knew the whole thing backward and forward and never had to be told anything except who we were supposed to be, and where we were supposed to stand.

". . . Joseph and Mary, his espoused wife, being great with child . . ."

"Pregnant!" yelled Ralph Herdman.

Well. That stirred things up. All the big kids began to giggle and all the little kids wanted to know what was so funny, and Mother had to hammer on the floor with a blackboard pointer. "That's enough, Ralph," she said, and went on with the story.

"I don't think it's very nice to say Mary was pregnant," Alice whispered to me.

"But she was," I pointed out. In a way, though, I agreed with her. It sounded too ordinary. Anybody could be pregnant. "Great with child" sounded better for Mary.

"I'm not supposed to talk about people being pregnant." Alice folded her hands in her lap and pinched her lips together. "I'd better tell my mother."

"Tell her what?"

"That your mother is talking about things like that in church. My mother might not want me to be here."

I was pretty sure she would do it. She wanted to be Mary, and she was mad at Mother. . . . But there wasn't much I could do about it, except pinch Alice, which I did. She yelped, and Mother separated us and made me sit beside Imogene Herdman. . . .

I wasn't crazy to sit next to Imogene—after all, I'd spent my whole life staying away from Imogene—but she didn't even notice me . . . not much, anyway.

"Shut up," was all she said. "I want to hear her."

I couldn't believe it. Among other things, the Herdmans were famous for never sitting still and never paying attention to anyone—teachers, parents (their own or anybody else's), the truant officer, the police—yet here they were, eyes glued on my mother and taking in every word.

"What's that?" they would yell whenever they didn't understand the language, and when Mother read about there being no room at the inn, Imogene's jaw dropped and she sat up in her seat.

"My God!" she said. "Not even for Jesus?"

I saw Alice purse her lips together so I knew that was something else Mrs. Wendleken would hear about—swearing in the church.

"Well, now, after all," Mother explained, "nobody knew the baby was going to turn out to be Jesus."

"You said Mary knew," Ralph said. "Why didn't she tell them?"

"*I* would have told them!" Imogene put in. "Boy, would I have told them! What was the matter with Joseph that he didn't tell them? Her pregnant and everything," she grumbled.

"What was that they laid the baby in?" Leroy said. "That manger . . . is that like a bed? Why would they have a bed in the barn?"

"That's just the point," Mother said. "They *didn't* have a bed in the barn, so Mary and Joseph had to use whatever there was. What would you do if you had a new baby and no bed to put the baby in?"

"We put Gladys in a bureau drawer," Imogene volunteered.

"Well, there you are," Mother said, blinking a little. "You didn't have a bed for Gladys so you had to use something else."

"Oh, we had a bed," Ralph said, "only Ollie was still in it and he wouldn't get out. He didn't like Gladys." . . .

"*Anyway,*" Mother said, "Mary and Joseph used the manger. A manger is a large wooden feeding trough for animals."

"What were the wadded-up clothes?" Claude wanted to know.

"The what?" Mother said.

"You read about it—'she wrapped him in wadded-up clothes.' "

"*Swaddling* clothes." Mother sighed. "Long ago, people used to wrap their babies very tightly in big pieces of material, so they couldn't move around. It made the babies feel cozy and comfortable."

I thought it probably just made the babies mad. Till then, I didn't know what swaddling clothes were either, and they sounded terrible, so I wasn't too surprised when Imogene got all excited about that.

"You mean they tied him up and put him in a feedbox?" she said. "Where was the Child Welfare?"

The Child Welfare was always checking up on the Herdmans. I'll bet if the Child Welfare had ever found Gladys all tied up in a bureau drawer they would have done something about it.

"And, lo, the Angel of the Lord came upon them," Mother went on, "and the glory of the Lord shone round about them, and—"

"Shazam!" Gladys yelled, flinging her arms out and smacking the kid next to her.

"What?" Mother said. Mother never read "Amazing Comics."

"Out of the black night with horrible vengeance, the Mighty Marvo—"

"I don't know what you're talking about, Gladys," Mother said. "This is the Angel of the Lord who comes to the shepherds in the fields, and—"

"Out of nowhere, right?" Gladys said. "In the black night, right?"

"Well . . ." Mother looked unhappy. "In a way."

So Gladys sat back down, looking very satisfied, as if this was at least one part of the Christmas story that made sense to her.

"Now when Jesus was born in Bethlehem of Judaea," Mother went on reading, "behold there came Wise Men from the East to Jerusalem, saying—"

"That's you, Leroy," Ralph said, "and Claude and Ollie. So pay attention."

"What does it mean, Wise Men?" Ollie wanted to know. "Were they like schoolteachers?"

"No, dumbbell," Claude said. "It means like President of the United States."

Mother looked surprised, and a little pleased—like she did when Charlie finally learned the times-tables up to five. "Why, that's very close, Claude," she said. "Actually, they were kings."

"Well, it's about time," Imogene muttered. "Maybe they'll tell the innkeeper where to get off, and get the baby out of the barn."

The great characters in story, in both Old and New Testaments, and in all the stories of all people written before and since, understand that reviling can indeed be a kind of praise. We cannot be angry at someone who is not there. When I am angry, the person toward whom I am angry is very present with me; I cannot avoid whoever it is.

The Herdmans got their own way, you might say, by taking over the best roles in the Christmas pageant. But who took over whom?

The Herdmans were always going to be Herdmans, but Herdmans with the difference that they were Herdmans who had encountered Love itself.

The children in Kenneth Grahame's *The Golden Age* were almost the opposite of the Herdmans. The Herdmans had nothing. Kenneth and his brothers had many books, many stories, so that when they chose to play King Arthur and the Knights of the Round Table, they were already familiar with the people and the adventures.

Kenneth is a normal boy from his day and place in history, but the charm and warmth we get from reading his story comes from the generosity which Kenneth shows, the delight with the day, with playing the game, rather than insisting on manipulating, controlling, getting his own way. The Herdmans had been given no lessons in courtesy. Courtesy came as spontaneously from Kenneth as it did from Scout. And because he was willing to give up having his own way, and let the others have the roles he would have chosen, the day was more alive and joyous and he himself had more fun than if he had sulked and insisted on being the star. Courtesy is never lukewarm.

We three younger ones were stretched at length in the orchard. The sun was hot, the season merry June, and never (I thought) had there been such wealth and riot of buttercups throughout the lush grass. Green-and-gold was the dominant key that day. Instead of active "pretence" with its shouts and its perspiration, how much better—I held—to lie at ease. . . . But the persistent Harold was not to be fobbed off.

"Well then," he began afresh, "let's pretend we're Knights of the Round Table; and (with a rush) *I'll* be Lancelot!"

"I won't play unless I'm Lancelot," I said. I didn't mean it really, but the game of Knights always began with this particular contest.

"Oh *please*," implored Harold. "You know when Edward's here I never get a chance of being Lancelot. I haven't been Lancelot for weeks!"

Then I yielded gracefully. "All right," I said. "I'll be Tristram."

"Oh, but you can't," cried Harold again. "Charlotte has always been Tristram. She won't play unless she's allowed to be Tristram! Be somebody else this time."

Charlotte said nothing, but breathed hard, looking straight before her. The peerless hunter and harper was her special hero of romance, and rather than see the part in less appreciative hands, she would have gone back in tears to the stuffy schoolroom.

"I don't care," I said: "I'll be anything. I'll be Sir Kay. Come on!"

Then once more in this country's story the mail-clad knights paced through the greenwood shaw, questing adventure, redressing wrong; and bandits, five to one, broke and fled discomfited to their caves. Once more were damsels rescued, dragons disembowelled, and giants, in every corner of the orchard, deprived of their already superfluous number of heads; while Palomides the Saracen waited for us by the well, and Sir Breuse Saunce Pité vanished in craven flight before the skilled spear that was his terror and his bane. Once more the lists were dight in Camelot, and all was gay with shimmer of silk and gold; the earth shook with thunder of hooves, ash-staves flew in splinters, and the firmament rang to the clash of sword on helm.

We cannot be fully alive without courage, and courage does not exist where there are no obstacles to surmount, nothing to fear. It takes courage for the baby to pull itself, staggering, to its feet, to take those first few tottering steps, to fall, pick itself up, and try again.

All through our lives we are called to be courageous. Emily must learn, earlier than many of us, to grieve, and to love and trust again after her father's death. Dorrie has to come to terms with her feelings about Fredlet. Alexis has to have the courage to take being called a coward.

We learn courage from each other, by seeing other people react to difficult and dangerous situations with courage, people we meet in real life, people we meet in story. Nowadays the people from whom we catch courage and openness and Naming are called role models. They used to be called heroes and heroines, and I think I'd rather be given courage by a hero or a heroine than by a role model. A hero or heroine can have a richer, more complex personality, be more contradictory than a role model.

Arthur and Lancelot have been heroes to many generations. They are depicted as fully human, and their very humanness caused them great grief. That doesn't make them any less heroes. We meet them again in *The Once and Future King* by T. H. White.

In the castle of Benwick, the French boy was looking at his face in the polished surface of a kettle-hat. It flashed in the sunlight with the stubborn gleam of metal. It was practically the same as the steel helmet which soldiers still wear, and it did not make a good mirror, but it was the best he could get. He turned the hat in various directions, hoping to get an average idea of his face from the different distortions which the bulges made. He was trying to find out what he was, and he was afraid of what he would find.

The boy thought that there was something wrong with him. All through his life—even when he was a great man with the world at his feet—he was to feel this gap: something at the bottom of his heart of which he was aware, and ashamed, but which he did not understand. There is no need for us to try to understand it. We do not have to dabble in a place which he preferred to keep secret.

The Armoury, where the boy stood, was lined with weapons of war. For the last two hours he had been whirling a pair of dumbbells in the air—he called them "poises"— . . . He was fifteen. He had just come back from England, where his father King Ban of Benwick had been helping the English King to quell a rebellion. You remember that Arthur wanted to catch his knights young, to train them for the Round Table, and that he had noticed Lancelot at the feast, because he was winning most of the games.

Lancelot, swinging his dumb-bells fiercely . . . had been remembering all the words of the only conversation which he had held with his hero.

The King had called him over when they were embarking for France—after he had kissed King Ban good-bye—and they had gone alone into a corner of the ship. The heraldic sails of Ban's fleet, and the sailors in the rigging, and the armed turrets and archers and seagulls, like flake-white, had been a background to their conversation.

"Lance," the King had said, "come here a moment, will you?"

"Sir."

"I was watching you playing games at the feast."

"Sir."

"You seemed to win most of them."

Lancelot squinted down his nose.

"I want to get hold of a lot of people who are good at games, to help with an idea I have. It is for the time when I am a real King, and have got this kingdom settled. I was wondering whether you would care to help, when you are old enough?"

The boy had made a sort of wriggle, and had suddenly flashed his eyes at the speaker.

"It is about knights," Arthur had continued. "I want to have an Order of Chivalry, like the Order of the Garter, which goes about fighting against Might. Would you like to be one of those?"

"Yes."

The King had looked at him closely, unable to see whether he was pleased or frightened or merely being polite.

"Do you understand what I am talking about?"

Lancelot had taken the wind out of his sails.

"We call it Fort Mayne in France," he had explained. "The man with the strongest arm in a clan gets made the head of it, and does what he pleases. That is why we call it Fort Mayne. You want to put an end to the Strong Arm, by having a band of knights who believe in justice rather than strength. Yes, I would like to be one of those very much. I must grow up first. Thank you. Now I must say good-bye."

So they had sailed away from England—the boy standing in the front of the ship and refusing to look back, because he did not want to show his feelings.

The prophets, such as Jonah or Elijah, to name two disparate ones, were very aware of the God with whom they were so angry. Ultimately, their anger had to be redeemed by being sacrificed— sacrifice in the old sense of the word: to make sacred. We cannot be really angry at someone we do not love deeply; it isn't worth the great expenditure of energy that anger takes otherwise. So when the anger is redeemed, it is sacrificed and made sacred.

In Ray Bradbury's *The Halloween Tree* many ordinary things are sacred. But so also are dark, strange things.

Joe Pipkin was the greatest boy who ever lived. The grandest boy who ever fell out of a tree and laughed at the joke. The finest boy who ever raced around the track, winning, and then seeing his friends a mile back somewhere, stumbled and fell, waited for them to catch up, and joined, breast and breast, breaking the winner's tape. The jolliest boy who ever hunted out all the haunted houses in town, which are hard to find, and came back to report on them and take all the kids to ramble through the basements and scramble up the ivy outside-bricks and shout down the chimneys and make water off the roofs, hooting and chimpanzee-dancing and ape-bellowing. The day Joe Pipkin was born all the Orange Crush and Nehi soda bottles in the world fizzed over; and joyful bees swarmed countrysides to sting maiden ladies. On his birthdays, the lake pulled out from the shore in midsummer and ran back with a tidal wave of boys, a big leap of bodies and a downcrash of laughs.

Dawns, lying in bed, you heard a birdpeck at the window. Pipkin.

You stuck your head out into the snow-water-clear-summer-morning air.

There in the dew on the lawn rabbit prints showed where, just a moment ago, not a dozen rabbits but one rabbit had circled and crisscrossed in a glory of life and exultation, bounding hedges, clipping ferns, tromping clover. It resembled the switchyards down at the rail depot. A million tracks in the grass but no . . .

Pipkin.

And here he rose up like a wild sunflower in the garden. His great round face burned with fresh sun. His eyes flashed Morse code signals:

"Hurry up! It's almost over!"

"What?"

"Today! Now! Six A.M. Dive down! *Wade* in it!"

Or: "This *summer!* Before you know, bang!—it's gone! Quick!"

And he sank away in sunflowers to come up all onions.

Pipkin, oh, dear Pipkin, finest and loveliest of boys.

How he ran so fast no one knew. His tennis shoes were ancient. They were colored green of forests jogged through, brown from old harvest trudges through September a year back, tar-stained from sprints along the docks and beaches where the coal barges came in, yellow from careless dogs, splinter-filled from climbing wood fences. His clothes were scarecrow clothes, worn by Pipkin's dogs all night, loaned to them for strolls through town, with chew marks along the cuffs and fall marks on the seat.

His hair? His hair was a great hedgehog bristle of bright brown-blond daggers sticking in all directions. His ears, pure peachfuzz. His hands, mittened with dust and the good smell of airedales and peppermint and stolen peaches from the far country orchards.

Pipkin. An assemblage of speeds, smells, textures; a cross section of all the boys who ever ran, fell, got up, and ran again.

No one, in all the years, had ever seen him sitting still. He was hard to remember in school, in one seat, for one hour. He was the last into the schoolhouse and the first exploded out when the bell ended the day.

Pipkin, sweet Pipkin.

Who yodeled and played the kazoo and hated girls more than all the other boys in the gang combined.

Pipkin, whose arm around your shoulder, and secret whisper of great doings this day, protected you from the world.

Pipkin.

God got up early just to see Pipkin come out of his house, like one of those people on a weatherclock. And the weather was always fine where Pipkin was.

Pipkin.

Caddie, in Rumer Godden's *The Battle of the Villa Fiorita,* is not a girl to look at the stars and yawn. She cries out when she is angry and unhappy, and she does something about it, even if that something involves sacrifice. When her mother has left her father, the only way that she and her brother, Hugh, can afford to go to bring their mother home again is to sell Caddie's beloved pony, Topaz.

He had everything planned: "We will tell Gwyneth I'm taking you down to Whitcross to say good-bye to Topaz before school," which was true, except the "before school." It was so reasonable that Gwyneth even gave them the money for their tickets.

Topaz was in a stall. Mr. Ringells had brought him in. "So your sister can see him," he told Hugh, and he said, "Nice little pony." Nice little pony!

"His legs are muddy," Caddie whispered to Hugh.

"They were muddy at Stebbings," but there was no denying Topaz was not the shining little pony he had been under her care. His coat was rough, his ears dusty. "I didn't leave a speck of dust on him." His feet were filled with caked mud and dung. "He will get thrush," she said severely to Mr. Ringells. He had water and hay and was quite plump, but, "Do you ever give him carrots?" Her eyes searched Mr. Ringells' face as if they would rake out of him what kind of man he was. "Apples or sugar?"

"He gets plenty of petting from the children. Never you fear," said Mr. Ringells, but Caddie did fear. "He will be a riding-school pony, not anybody's own," she said.

She spoke once in the train on the way back. "He's used to being loved. What will he *think?*" and Hugh gave her a piece of advice. "For people, it's much better never to think what animals must be thinking." Then he did something that Caddie had only known him do once before; he put his arm round her and squeezed her. Long ago, on the day he went to that first school, suddenly turning from the car, he had run back and given Caddie a violent wordless hug. The small far-away Caddie had been filled with love and wonder. In the Whitcross train she felt nothing at all.

Now, on the villa terrace, it was Fanny who was weeping. She had jumped up. "Caddie, we must get Topaz back, make Mr. Ringells sell him back to us. Rob and I will have a house soon and probably in the country. We will buy Topaz back, wherever he is, and keep him for you. I promise," but the figure bowed in the chair at the end of the table never moved and Rob stopped Fanny. "I should leave her alone just now."

"But you don't know what this means, Rob."

"I can guess."

"Hugh, how could you? How could you?"

"What do you mean, how could I?" Hugh's head came up. He looked fierce. "It wasn't I who made Caddie sell Topaz," he said. "It was you."

"Precisely," said Rob before Fanny could cry out. They were getting into a tangle of emotions and he made the words brisk. "All the same, we mustn't promise what we can't do. By the time we find a house, Caddie may be too big for a pony and . . ." but Fanny could not bear the way Caddie sat silently bowed in the chair.

She broke away from Rob, and went to Caddie, kneeling down by her. "Perhaps we can't buy Topaz back," she said. "But I shall never forget, never, what you have done to get to me. To sell Topaz." Fanny's voice was broken. "And that long long journey." She held out her hand to Hugh. "Oh my darlings, if you knew what it means . . . that you ran away to me."

Hugh was silent but Caddie raised an indignant face. "We *didn't* run away to you," said Caddie. "We came to fetch you."

Caddie has to give up the animal she loves. For Miyax in *Julie of the Wolves* by Jean Craighead George, it is the other way round. Instead of leaving the wolves, she must, as far as humanly possible, learn their way of communicating with each other, learn their ways of expressing love, which may be very different from the ways she is used to.

In some societies, holding out the hand, as we do, to shake it, is a gesture of aggression, to be met with by aggression.

Miyax must be very careful in each movement she makes, that it is interpreted according to her intent. We have become overcasual in our rituals of greeting and leavetaking, blessing and even reviling. We focus on our own gesture, rather than on the need, intent, response of the other.

I learned a great deal from Miyax.

The scribes and Pharisees tended to look at people and see where they ought to be. Jesus looked at people and saw where they were.

Amaroq got to his feet, and as he slowly arose he seemed to fill the sky and blot out the sun. He was enormous. He could swallow her without even chewing.

"But he won't," she reminded herself. "Wolves do not eat people. That's gussak talk. Kapugen said wolves are gentle brothers."

The black puppy was looking at her and wagging his tail. Hopefully, Miyax held out a pleading hand to him. His tail wagged harder. The mother rushed to him and stood above him sternly. When he licked her cheek apologetically, she pulled back her lips from her fine white teeth. They flashed as she smiled and forgave her cub. . . .

The reprimanded pup snapped at a crane fly and shook himself. Bits of lichen and grass spun off his fur. He reeled unsteadily, took a wider stance, and looked down at his sleeping sister. With a yap he jumped on her and rolled her to her feet. She whined. He barked and picked up a bone. When he was sure she was watching, he ran down the slope with it. The sister tagged after him. He stopped and she grabbed the bone, too. She pulled; he pulled; then he pulled and she yanked.

Miyax could not help laughing. The puppies played with bones like Eskimo children played with leather ropes.

"I understand *that*," she said to the pups. "That's tug-o-war. Now how do you say, 'I'm hungry'?"

Amaroq was pacing restlessly along the crest of the frost heave as if something were about to happen. His eyes shot to Silver, then to the gray wolf Miyax had named Nails. These glances seemed to be a summons, for Silver and Nails glided to him, spanked the ground with their forepaws and bit him gently under the chin. He wagged his tail furiously and took Silver's slender nose in his mouth. She crouched before him, licked his cheek and lovingly bit his lower jaw. Amaroq's tail flashed high as her mouthing charged him with vitality. He nosed her affectionately. Unlike the fox, who met his mate only in the breeding season, Amaroq lived with his mate all year.

Next, Nails took Amaroq's jaw in his mouth and the leader bit the top of his nose. A third adult, a small male, came slinking up. He got down on his belly before Amaroq, rolled trembling to his back, and wriggled.

"Hello, Jello," Miyax whispered, for he reminded her of the quivering gussak dessert her mother-in-law made.

She had seen the wolves mouth Amaroq's chin twice before and so she concluded that it was a ceremony, a sort of "Hail to the Chief." He must indeed be their leader for he was clearly the wealthy wolf; that is, wealthy as she had known the meaning of the word on Nunivak Island. There the old Eskimo hunters she had known in her childhood thought the riches of life were intelligence, fearlessness, and love. A man with these gifts was rich and was a great spirit who was admired in the same way that the gussaks admired a man with money and goods. . . .

Amaroq wailed again, stretching his neck until his head was high above the others. They gazed at him affectionately and it was plain to see that he was their great spirit, a royal leader who held his group together with love and wisdom.

Any fear Miyax had of the wolves was dispelled by their affection for each other. They were friendly animals and so devoted to Amaroq that she needed only to be accepted by him to be accepted by all. She even knew how to achieve this—bite him under the chin. But how was she going to do that?

She studied the pups, hoping they had a simpler way of expressing their love for him. The black puppy approached the leader, sat, then lay down and wagged his tail vigorously. He gazed up at Amaroq in pure adoration, and the royal eyes softened. . . .

Miyax hunched forward on her elbows, the better to see and learn. She now knew how to be a good puppy, pay tribute to the leader, and even to be a leader by biting others on the top of the nose.

Miyax got on all fours and looked for the nearest pup to speak to. It was Sister.

"Ummmm," she whined, and when Sister turned around she narrowed her eyes and showed her white teeth. Obediently, Sister lay down.

"I'm talking wolf! I'm talking wolf!" Miyax clapped, and tossing her head like a pup, crawled in a happy circle. As she was coming back she saw all five puppies sitting in a row watching her, their heads cocked in curiosity. Boldly the black pup came toward her, his fat backside swinging as he trotted to the bottom of her frost heave, and barked.

"You are *very* fearless and *very* smart," she said. "Now I know why you are special. You are wealthy and the leader of the puppies. There is no doubt what you'll grow up to be. So I shall name you after my father Kapugen, and I shall call you Kapu for short." . . . Sliding back to her camp, she heard the grass swish and looked up to see Amaroq and his hunters sweep around her frost heave and stop about five feet away. She could smell the sweet scent of their fur.

The hairs on her neck rose and her eyes widened. Amaroq's ears went forward aggressively and she remembered that wide eyes meant fear to him. It was not good to show him she was afraid. Animals attacked the fearful. She tried to narrow them, but remembered that was not right either. Narrowed eyes were mean. In

desperation she recalled that Kapu had moved forward when chal-
lenged. She pranced right up to Amaroq. Her heart beat furiously as
she grunt-whined the sound of the puppy begging adoringly for
attention. Then she got down on her belly and gazed at him with
fondness.

The great wolf backed up and avoided her eyes. She had said
something wrong! Perhaps even offended him. Some slight gesture
that meant nothing to her had apparently meant something to the
wolf. His ears shot forward angrily and it seemed all was lost. She
wanted to get up and run, but she gathered her courage and pranced
closer to him. Swiftly she patted him under the chin.

The signal went off. It sped through his body and triggered
emotions of love. Amaroq's ears flattened and his tail wagged in
friendship. He could not react in any other way to the chin pat, for the
roots of this signal lay deep in wolf history. It was inherited from
generations and generations of leaders before him. As his eyes
softened, the sweet odor of ambrosia arose from the gland on the top
of his tail and she was drenched lightly in wolf scent. Miyax was one
of the pack.

One of the early stories that brought joy and courage and added
awareness to me was another wolf story, Rudyard Kipling's tale of
Mowgli in *The Jungle Books*. There's nothing lukewarm about
Mother Wolf's response to a threat to her human baby.

The bushes rustled a little in the thicket, and Father Wolf dropped
with his haunches under him, ready for his leap. Then, if you had
been watching, you would have seen the most wonderful thing in the
world—the wolf checked in mid-spring. He made his bound before he
saw what it was he was jumping at, and then he tried to stop himself.
The result was that he shot up straight into the air for four or five feet,
landing almost where he left ground.

"Man!" he snapped. "A man's cub. Look!"

Directly in front of him, holding on by a low branch, stood a naked
brown baby who could just walk—as soft and as dimpled a little atom
as ever came to a wolf's cave at night. He looked up into Father
Wolf's face, and laughed.

"Is that a man's cub?" said Mother Wolf. "I have never seen one.
Bring it here."

A wolf accustomed to moving his own cubs can, if necessary,
mouth an egg without breaking it, and though Father Wolf's jaws

closed right on the child's back not a tooth even scratched the skin, as he laid it down among the cubs.

"How little! How naked, and—how bold!" said Mother Wolf, softly. The baby was pushing his way between the cubs to get close to the warm hide. "Ahai! He is taking his meal with the others. And so this is a man's cub. Now, was there ever a wolf that could boast of a man's cub among her children?"

"I have heard now and again of such a thing, but never in our Pack or in my time," said Father Wolf. "He is altogether without hair, and I could kill him with a touch of my foot. But see, he looks up and is not afraid." . . .

"Shere Khan does us great honor," said Father Wolf, but his eyes were very angry. "What does Shere Khan need?"

"My quarry. A man's cub went this way," said Shere Khan. "Its parents have run off. Give it to me." . . .

"The Wolves are a free people," said Father Wolf. "They take orders from the Head of the Pack, and not from any striped cattle-killer. The man's cub is ours—to kill if we choose." . . .

The tiger's roar filled the cave with thunder. Mother Wolf shook herself clear of the cubs and sprang forward. . . .

The moonlight was blocked out of the mouth of the cave, for the great square head and shoulders [of Shere Khan, the tiger] were thrust into the entrance.

"The man's cub is mine. . . . He shall not be killed. He shall live to run with the Pack and to hunt with the Pack; and in the end, look you, hunter of little naked cubs—frog-eater—fish-killer—he shall hunt *thee!* "

He came to my desk with quivering lip—
  The lesson was done.
"Dear Teacher, I want a new leaf," he said,
  "I have spoiled this one."
I took the old leaf, stained and blotted,
And gave him a new one, all unspotted,
  And into his sad eyes smiled,
  "Do better now, my child!"

Anonymous

3

The New Leaf

Our ability to marvel at the glory of the stars, to cry out at suffering, to bless, and to revile comes from our encounters with other people. I didn't always have teachers who were willing to give me a new page when I'd ruined the old one, and those teachers who refused to let me try again were unNamers, were Annihilators.

The teachers who Named me, helped me out of the mud, laughed lovingly, called me Maddening, were not always the teachers in the classroom. Everyone we encounter is a teacher. For Miyax and Mowgli, wolves were teachers. For Kenneth, the knights of King Arthur were teachers. For Melissa, in Isabelle Holland's *Heads You Win, Tails I Lose,* it was Miss Peabody and Miss Ainslie.

Ted, a handsome but self-satisfied high school student, has been told by the librarian either to stay in the library and study or to go talk somewhere else.

Ted, thinking himself safe behind a stack of books, put his thumb to his nose. There were more giggles from those who could see. Among them was Miss Peabody whom he had forgotten and who didn't giggle.

"Ah yes, Ted," she said loudly. "A gesture known and used internationally. But I don't think Mrs. Summers had a chance to appreciate it. Stand up, now, and do it again."

It was one of those things that could have gone either way. Given his good looks and popularity, Ted could have done it with panache and made the librarian and the teacher look silly.

But Mrs. Summers was liked and respected and Miss Peabody had her own standing as a kind of brilliant kook.

"Yes, do, Ted. I'm sorry I missed it." Mrs. Summers sat back, a look of amusement on her elegant, wise face under the gray hair. "Don't keep us waiting."

My misery lightened considerably as Ted, brick red, rose to his feet, did a hasty retake of the gesture and sat down again.

"Thank you. Now we can all go back to work again. That is, if you will allow us."

Later, Miss Peabody gives Melissa a ride home.

Miss Peabody and I talked about school, which had just started, the drama club for which she was consultant, and the play which she wanted us to do.

"Why *Antigone*?" I asked.

"It's a good play. Have you read it?"

"No. And I know some of the other kids in the club have other ideas about what we ought to do. Something more modern. More relevant."

Miss Peabody moaned. "Relevant! It used to be such a nice word. It had impact. Now it's just a cliché."

"Well, you know what I mean, Miss Peabody."

"I do. And I think you'll find *Antigone* very relevant."

"What's it about?"

"Well, it's about principle versus political compromise. Can you think of anything more relevant?"

I grinned in the dark.

"Read it, Melissa, and see for yourself."

"All right."

We drove for a while in silence, which is something that can be very pleasant. No demands, no wondering what the other person is thinking and how soon they're going to pounce or what improvement they're about to point out you can make on yourself.

As we turned back into the town and neared my street Miss Peabody suddenly said, "Ted MacDonald will probably be a reasonable and pleasant human being in about a dozen years' time if—but only if—he's lucky enough to have a few ego-deflating experiences between now and then. But until that happens he will remain the good-looking insensitive block we all know and endure."

We drew up in front of my house. She leaned on her steering wheel and gently revved Ferdinand a few times. "And if you quote me on any of that, Melissa, I'll deny it all." She turned. "When you next feel like you're going into a depression over what King Ted, or anyone, thinks of you, why don't you turn it around and see what you think—*think,* not just feel—about him or her or it or them? It has a very exhilarating effect. More heads have been taken out of more ovens doing that. Gently with Ferdinand's door. Don't slam it. Read

Antigone. I want you to have a part in the play. No—don't argue. Good night."

Because of Miss Peabody's urging, and her faith in Melissa, when *Antigone* is cast, Melissa does have a role. So, of course, does Ted. After the cast has been chosen, Miss Ainslie, the director, calls them together.

"I want to talk to you about the play. I said it was about civil rights and tyranny. But it is also—mainly—about what the Greeks call hubris, which means pride or arrogance, and how the gods punish anyone who is guilty of it, as Creon is. He defies a law of the gods, a divine law, in favor of what he thinks is the good of the state, and in a fascinating, logical sequence of events, destroys everything he loves and values most. It's a play about law in cause and effect, about the clash of wills between Creon, the state, and Antigone, the rebel, who is yet obedient to divine law. It's about justice. It's one of the great plays of the world and it deserves everything you've got."

With teachers like Miss Peabody and Miss Ainslie, it is no wonder that Melissa is able to turn over a new leaf. But sometimes there are people, often children, who are not only not given a new leaf, they aren't given any leaf at all. Sometimes they wither and die, like many children in the slums of our big cities, hooked as toddlers on drugs, life taken away from them before it has even begun.

But sometimes, sometimes there springs up in the wilderness, faith and courage against tremendous odds. The story of Tomorrow Billy in *The Planet of Junior Brown* by Virginia Hamilton is an extraordinary affirmation of the power of the human spirit to survive and even to flourish in places where that would seem impossible.

There is no place where Christ cannot work, no odds too great.

Buddy heard everything. He captured the sounds of outside and held them in his memory. If they changed at all, if footsteps were added, if any part of the traffic flow at the corner slowed or turned into the street, he knew it.

Buddy could distinguish sound. But he had not known sound at all when he was the size of the younger boy whom he held onto now. When he was that age, about nine, he had stumbled upon a vacant building all boarded up. And climbing to the top floor of the building to escape the people from the Children's Shelter, Buddy had come upon that unbelievable world of homeless children. There had been six or seven young boys and one bigger boy in that boarded-up tenement. When Buddy came upon them, none of them had moved. The bigger boy had been sitting on his haunches, his every muscle ready for battle if a fight were needed.

They all had looked at Buddy. It had been the bigger boy who motioned him to come forward, who had given him a bowl of soup to eat.

"This is the planet of Tomorrow Billy," the bigger boy had told Buddy. "If you want to live on it, you can."

Buddy remembered he had feared the bigger boy at first, even when he had decided to stay. He had been afraid they were crazy addicts, or that the big boy forced the others to steal for him.

The bigger boy had told Buddy, "If you stay with us, you'll do as I say to do. There're no parents here. We are together only to survive. Each one of us must live, not for the other," the boy had said. "The highest law is to learn to live for yourself. I'm the one to teach you how to do that and I'll take care of you just as long as you need me to. I'm Tomorrow Billy."

In the dark of the basement, remembering that time, Buddy smiled to himself. He scooted along the floor, moving the two boys with him until he reached the wall in front of the mountain of debris. There Buddy released them. They moved quietly until they were sitting with their backs against the basement wall.

There was a low table next to the two boys. Buddy found the one patio candle on it and lit it. The weak light seemed suddenly bright to the boys' unaccustomed eyes. Buddy sat on his knees with his palms flat on the table top, staring into the candlelight.

How many Tomorrow Billys had there been, and for how long? It had taken Buddy three years to learn all that the bigger boy on his planet could teach him. Each night, the boy came to where the group lived high up in the tenement. When he had taught them and fed them and furnished them what clothing they needed, he would prepare to leave them again. Always they'd ask him, "Tomorrow, Billy? Will we see you again tomorrow night?" The boy had always answered yes. But one time, after about three years, they'd somehow forgot to ask the question. Tomorrow Billy had never returned. The group had broken up then. Long after each had gone his separate way, Buddy realized why the boy had not returned. It was not that they had forgotten to ask the question, "Tomorrow, Billy?" It was that they no longer needed to.

Turning from the candlelight, Buddy surveyed the two boys against the wall. Their eyes hadn't left his face. He recognized the older of the two to be one of the few kids he had passed along to be part of a group down on Gansevoort Street in the West Village.

Under Buddy's steady gaze, the boy thought to tell Buddy his name. "I'm Franklin Moore," he said. "You may remember me as Russell. That was my real name, the one I had when I first came here."

Buddy laughed inwardly. It was a strange dude who would change his name from Russell to Franklin. But it was a rule that a boy moving from one planet to another would have to change his name.

"I don't want to know your real name," Buddy told him. "Keep it to yourself, if you need to. But try to forget it, if you're really Franklin Moore."

The boy said nothing. He was quick to learn and his mind clicked in time with what Buddy had just revealed to him about himself.

"Were you told to come up here?" Buddy asked him.

"Tomorrow Billy down there say to come up and bring this kid here because they are full up and you suppose to be just through with one group."

Buddy listened closely to Franklin Moore. The boy could be a thief, stumbling on the group the way Buddy himself had years ago. No. Once you start suspecting them, you'll end by giving them passwords to get in. You'll have to put them in uniforms so you'll know who belongs. You'll next distrust anyone who might forget the password or has his uniform stolen.

"What's your name?" Buddy asked the younger boy. The boy was small and yellow-skinned. His hair was freshly cut and washed and he wore clean clothes.

It took the boy some minutes to come up with a name. He had been taught for however long he had some parent to teach him that his name was who he was.

"Look," Buddy told him. "If you want to use the name you were born with, okay, because I'll never know the difference. See, I can't get inside your head so maybe you make up the name and maybe you don't, it's all right. But dig, it's better you give up the name you were born with. See, because just having a last name the same as the mama or aunt or daddy you once knew reminds you of them. And remembering is going to make you feel pretty bad sometimes when maybe Franklin here or anybody else, either, isn't around to make you feel better."

The boy still hadn't said anything. Every now and then he peeked shyly at Buddy. Clearly he was in awe of his Tomorrow Billy.

"I think maybe he might be hungry," Franklin told Buddy. "We had to do some hurrying. I found him out on the street begging. Some drunk had got hold on him and was making him work for him."

"You have to stone the drunk to get the kid away?" Buddy asked.

"Nothing like that!" Franklin said. He looked shocked but then he understood that Buddy had been testing him.

"I gave him enough money to satisfy the drunk," Franklin said. "When the drunk had his wine, I just disappeared with the kid."

"Good," Buddy said.

"Time we get over to the house on Gansevoort, it's getting late," Franklin continued, "and I know I've got to get him stashed before night. So they get him cleaned up there and cut his hair—but he didn't eat because we had to get up here while I can still see the ladder good enough to get him down it."

Franklin sighed, glancing at the child next to him. He had already grown somewhat protective of the boy. It was always a pleasant surprise for Buddy to see how quickly an older boy became attached to a younger one. Always the younger one would grow up better able to take care of himself than the older one had been.

"I guess maybe you are hungry too, just the same as the kid," Buddy said to Franklin.

Franklin stared down at his hands, fearing his hunger would appear selfish.

"Nothing wrong with needing to eat, man," Buddy told him.

Buddy moved to the edge of the candlelight. In the shadows there stood a double-door file cabinet. Buddy unlocked it and opened it; there were stacks of clothing on the upper shelf and a supply of towels and soap. Canned goods, staples, plates and cooking and eating utensils were kept on the two lower shelves. On top of the cabinet were quarts of bottled water and a Sterno set.

Buddy lifted down the Sterno and water and set them on the table. He took from the cabinet a can of soup, a loaf of dark bread, powdered milk, two bananas and a can of tuna fish.

The boys watched eagerly as Buddy spread the food out on the table. "Yea!" he said happily. The boys scooted forward to help.

Opening the bottled water was like a ritual. The younger boy was allowed to do it. When he had used the opener properly in order to get the bottle top off, he leaned back, satisfied.

From a drawer in the table, Buddy produced three small paper cups. "Now," he said to the younger boy. "You'll pour a half a cup of water in each of the cups. You can drink it that way or you can mix it with milk. If you mix it with milk, you can have more if you want. But if you have only water," Buddy said, "you can have just a half a cup.

We buy the water, so it's precious in the wintertime with all the water fountains turned off."

The younger boy would have his water mixed in with milk so he could have a second cup. He poured out the water, clutching the large bottle tightly in both hands. When the task was done, he forced the top back on the bottle. He passed the bottle to Franklin, who, when he was finished, passed it on to Buddy. Buddy returned the bottle to its place on top of the file cabinet.

They ate tuna fish sandwiches. They had hot soup followed by banana slices. All of the food tasted wonderfully good.

Softly the younger boy spoke. "I got a name for myself," he said.

Buddy was chewing, so he didn't say anything. The boy stared up at him with wide, happy eyes.

"So what is it, what's your name?" Franklin asked.

"Nightman," the boy said.

There was a dead silence, after which Franklin said, "Naw! That's not a name!"

"How come it's not?" Buddy asked him, for the younger boy had looked crestfallen. "Take a name like Malcolm, Malcolm X. Now that's an opinion when you think about it. But a cat's got a right to his opinion."

"Well, is Nightman a first name or a last name?" Franklin asked the boy.

"It's a first name," the boy told him. "My name is Nightman Black."

Buddy had to smile at the kid. The kid had made peace with the dark by making himself a part of it. "That's a good, tough name," Buddy told him. "Nightman, you are real together."

After the dishes were cleaned and put away, and the cabinet locked again, the three of them sat against the basement wall. Buddy talked quickly but calmly to the two boys. He spoke particularly to Nightman Black. It would be hard for him to catch on at first, Buddy told him. Nightman would naturally go to the sections of town where there were black people. That was all right so long as he stayed out of bars, so long as he kept himself moving. Don't stand on street corners, Buddy told him. The best place to rest was in playgrounds but only at lunchtime and after three o'clock. He wouldn't be going to school for another week or two. Buddy told Nightman that he couldn't go to school until he was safe being on his own. Because until he could get by, he would be nervous. He'd want to go home with the first teacher who was nice to him. Nightman might blurt out the fact that he didn't have a home. He might tell some kid that he had to sleep in a broken-down building. No, Nightman had to get behind living for himself; and when he could do that, he would have no trouble in school or anywhere else.

To grow up surrounded by books of fantasy, fairy tales, myths means to grow up with an awareness of mystery and wonder, and to be unafraid of those marvels beyond the limited realm of fact.

It seems extraordinary to me that we human beings have a tendency to pay attention to a good which is distorted, and think that thereby the original good has been destroyed. All good things can become sour or rotten. But a wormy apple does not mean that we should refuse to eat the perfect apple from the tree.

There is a lot of emphasis today, particularly among the more extreme right branches of the church, on the evils of witchcraft. Any book that mentions witches, or magic, or ghosts is automatically to be taken from the shelves. What, then, are we to do with the story of the witch of Endor and Samuel's ghost? Must we remove the Bible from the shelves because it contains not only ghosts and witches but incest and murder and lust and rape? We human beings tend to distort and misuse, if not abuse, the original goodness of creation, but that does not make the original good less good, nor the marvelousness less marvelous.

In Ursula Le Guin's *A Wizard of Earthsea,* Ged's teacher understands this. "You must not change one thing, one pebble, one grain of sand, until you know what good and evil will follow on that act."

It would seem that Ged is being taught to honor creation, as Adam and Eve were expected to honor all that was in the garden.

If we are to keep our planet, we must regain our ability to honor it and to treat it with love and respect.

Part of each day he studied with the Master Chanter, learning the Deeds of heroes and the Lays of wisdom, beginning with the oldest of all songs, the *Creation of Éa.* Then with a dozen other lads he would practise with the Master Windkey at arts of wind and weather. Whole bright days of spring and early summer they spent out in Roke Bay in light catboats, practising steering by word, and stilling waves, and speaking to the world's wind, and raising up the magewind. These are very intricate skills, and frequently Ged's head got whacked by the swinging boom as the boat jibed under a wind suddenly blowing backwards, or his boat and another collided though they had the whole bay to navigate in, or all three boys in his boat went swimming unexpectedly as the boat was swamped by a huge, unintended wave. There were quieter expeditions ashore, other days, with the Master Herbal who taught the ways and properties of things that grow; and the Master Hand taught sleight and jugglery and the lesser arts of Changing.

At all these studies Ged was apt, and within a month was bettering lads who had been a year at Roke before him. Especially the tricks of illusion came to him so easily that it seemed he had been born knowing them and needed only to be reminded. The Master Hand was a gentle and lighthearted old man, who had endless delight in the wit and beauty of the crafts he taught; Ged soon felt no awe of him, but asked him for this spell and that spell, and always the Master smiled and showed him what he wanted. But one day, having it in mind to put Jasper to shame at last, Ged said to the Master Hand in the Court of Seeming, "Sir, all these charms are much the same; knowing one, you know them all. And as soon as the spell-weaving ceases, the illusion vanishes. Now if I make a pebble into a diamond"—and he did so with a word and a flick of his wrist—"what must I do to make that diamond remain diamond? How is the changing-spell locked, and made to last?"

The Master Hand looked at the jewel that glittered on Ged's palm, bright as the prize of a dragon's hoard. The old Master murmured one word, *"Tolk,"* and there lay the pebble, no jewel but a rough grey bit of rock. The Master took it and held it out on his own hand. "This is a rock; *tolk* in the True Speech," he said, looking mildly up at Ged now. "A bit of the stone of which Roke Isle is made, a little bit of the dry land on which men live. It is itself. It is part of the world. By the Illusion-Change you can make it look like a diamond—or a flower or a fly or an eye or a flame—" The rock flickered from shape to shape as he named them, and returned to rock. "But that is mere seeming. Illusion fools the beholder's senses; it makes him see and hear and feel that the thing is changed. But it does not change the thing. To change this rock into a jewel, you must change its true name. And to do that, my son, even to so small a scrap of the world, is to change the world. It can be done. Indeed it can be done. It is the art of the Master Changer, and you will learn it, when you are ready to learn it. But you must not change one thing, one pebble, one grain of sand, until you know what good and evil will follow on that act. The world is in balance, in Equilibrium. A wizard's power of Changing and of Summoning can shake the balance of the world. It is dangerous, that power. It is most perilous. It must follow knowledge, and serve need. To light a candle is to cast a shadow. . . ."

He looked down at the pebble again. "A rock is a good thing, too, you know," he said, speaking less gravely. "If the Isles of Earthsea were all made of diamond, we'd lead a hard life here. Enjoy illusions, lad, and let the rocks be rocks."

There are miracles everywhere, and they are our teachers, too. The miracle of snowflakes always fills me with awe and joy. That not one single snow crystal is ever exactly like any other, that every snowflake is completely and forever unique, is a great and glorious miracle. So is the miracle that not one single human being is ever exactly like any other human being anywhere.

Sometimes we are given the miraculousness of life by unexpected teachers, a convict, for instance, let out of prison only because he is dying.

Mister Beck, in Malcolm J. Bosse's *The 79 Squares*, shows Eric a world of wonder he never suspected.

In half an hour, following instructions, Eric had completed the task of cutting the string into four lengths and tying them to pegs of poplar branches. Next to the old man's chair he stretched out the string, sunk the pegs into the ground, and measured the distance between them with his steel tape. The string and pegs outlined a square, six feet by six feet.

"Good," said Mister Beck with pursed lips. "Now take the whole thing over to the southwest corner and peg it down."

Eric did. He studied the space enclosed by the white lines stretched tight between the pegs.

"Now climb inside," Mister Beck commanded.

Eric turned quizzically. "Climb inside?"

"That's what I said. Climb inside that square and sit down."

Eric did.

Sitting with his back toward the square, Mister Beck had to crane his neck around to see Eric. "Stay inside there one hour. Then pull the pegs up along one side and move them over to make an adjoining square. Got that?"

Eric nodded.

"Then climb inside that new square and stay one hour."

Mister Beck was facing straight ahead, so he no longer saw Eric. It seemed to Eric that the old man had turned away as an act of faith; it was like saying he trusted Eric to follow orders without being watched. "One square after another," Mister Beck continued, "until you cover the whole garden. Seventy-nine squares of it." . . .

"But—" Eric looked around wildly. He felt as though someone had just slammed the door, shutting him in a dark closet. "What am I supposed to *do* in here?"

"What do you think?"

"I don't know."

"You're in there for one hour. What are you going to do about it?" Mister Beck asked sharply.

"I don't know!"

"I thought we agreed about you looking at the garden."

"Well, yes—"

"So do it. Look at it. Look inside the six feet of it belonging to you right now."

"What belongs to me?"

"The six-foot square you're inhabiting. For the next hour it's the whole damn world!" . . . .

Eric glanced at his crossed legs, his jeans, his tennis shoes, at his hands playing idly across the top of the grass. Was he crazy to do this? . . .

He surveyed the whole plot of ground within the white lines. His kingdom? Nuts. He flopped down violently on his stomach, the way he used to do as a small boy when he wanted to pout. He placed his cheek flat against the earth, as he had done yesterday to look at the ant. He eyed the grass from the distance of an inch. Soon a tiny insect alit on a blade of grass; it came out of nowhere, a green nub of a thing. Had he failed to see it alight, Eric would not have taken it for anything alive. He stared at the little bump on the blade of grass until he couldn't tell if it was part of the grass or really a living thing clinging there. But when he blinked, during the instant his eyes were closed, the bump disappeared. The insect was gone. . . .

There was a buzz near his left ear, so he flicked wildly at the side of his head. Something flashed like tinfoil, dipped toward the earth, and vanished. More buzzing. There were restless things everywhere. . . .

A faint stir of wind agitated the branches, forming sudden intricate designs of leaf and twig against the flat blue background. Something moved on a branch. It was an ant, moving along the stem and over the joint of each leaf. Like a physical blow, the thought came to Eric that the world of an ant was small. Of course, he had always known this, but somehow it was new to him now. Where leaf fitted into branch, there was a large bump—at least to the ant—like a huge mound of thick solder looming ahead that must be traversed, as the ant journeyed endlessly along the road leading to the far distant bottom of the valley where the immense trunk of the privet bush sunk its huge roots into the earth. The ant's feelers kept tapping. The insect must not see very well or far, and it had that great journey to take before reaching solid ground. For a couple of seconds Eric felt as though he lived in the black skull of that tiny creature, peering from its globular eyes at the gigantic world.

Then the magic moments passed. Eric sat up again and glanced aimlessly at privet bush, grass, strings, at the figure obscured by the back of the chair. . . . How long had he been in the square? Eric had sworn to himself not to look at his watch, but curiosity was too much for him—he raised his wrist and in shocked dismay realized that only twenty minutes had gone by. He had expected—had hoped—for much longer. He just might not hold out for a full hour if he didn't find something to do, so he decided to play a game to pass the time.

He would take a census of his country. Crawling to one corner of the square, he began to count anything that was alive. Some time later—he did not glance at his watch—he lost count at about fifty insects; there were just too many of them passing in view for him to keep track. . . . Then he gave up the game altogether, because his interest shifted . . . to the very real life going on down there at ground level. He knelt and looked until his back ached from the strain of holding such a tense position. He had never examined anything in his life as closely as he did the little patch of earth within four pieces of string.

Ged was taught a reverence for all that is, and that it must be treated with love, caution, and wonder. The trembling of the first star in the sky at night is always a sign of hope. A smile, following tears, is always a sign of reconciliation. How can we ever look at the sunset and not see its beauty? But we do. One of the diseases to afflict this century is a loss of wonder. We cannot revere creation if we have lost our wonder about it.

Miss Blue, in M. E. Kerr's *Is That You, Miss Blue?*, was, perhaps, as odd a teacher as Mister Beck, but each of them, in their completely different ways, taught superbly because of their own reverence for creation.

The great teachers, be they parents, wolves, children, convicts, cranks, mice, pigs, cherubim—the list is infinite—have retained their sense of wonder.

Miss Blue's science class was the last class of the day. Only Miss Blue could hold anyone's attention at that hour, and her way of doing it was not as much teaching as it was dramatizing.

Take the afternoon in early November, for example, when Miss Blue began by walking across to the window, staring out for a while as though she'd forgotten we were there, and then without turning around to face us, she said, "On a cloudy, rainy day exactly like this one, in the year 1896, a Frenchman put something away in a drawer, until a sunny day should come along."

Then she turned and looked at us. "And because of just such a day as this, and because the Frenchman didn't know that he wouldn't need sunlight for what he'd planned, we had a discovery. What was it?"

"Was it radium?" Ditty Hutt asked.

"Not yet. It was a step in that direction."

"It was radioactive material," said Ditty, the only one who knew what Miss Blue was leading up to (because her father was a scientist); "it was Antoine Becquerel who put a piece of uranium ore in his desk drawer. He thought it was phosphorescent, and he wanted to see if, when he exposed it to sunlight, he could use its light to make a photograph."

"Correct," said Miss Blue. "Becquerel put his carefully wrapped photographic plates into the desk drawer with the uranium ore. When a sunny day came, he took them out . . . and what did he discover?"

"He found the plates all fogged," said Ditty, "as if they'd been exposed to sunlight. He realized some kind of radiation was coming out of the ore, and it didn't matter if the ore had been exposed to sunlight or not."

Miss Blue then ran to the blackboard, her cross swinging back and forth across her bosom, while she drew the outlines of two large heads, a man's and a woman's. These were associates of Becquerel.

"They took over where he left off !!" Miss Blue shouted excitedly. "Who will fill in their names?"

Before the hour and a half was up, there were not only the names of Pierre Curie and Marie Sklodowska Curie across the faces, there were formulas and dates drawn in various colors of chalk, and there were other outlines of faces, other names like Sir J. J. Thomson, Sir Ernest Rutherford, et cetera, and suddenly I knew about atoms and about alpha, beta, and gamma rays, and I'd even forgotten it was Miss Blue up there, crazy Miss Blue from the closet on David Copperfield, making *me,* hater of science and dunce about all things scientific, actually making me interested in all that.

It wasn't the first time it had happened. She'd also hooked me into listening about Newton's system with my mouth hanging open in wonder, as well as the theories of Copernicus, Galileo, and Archimedes. I wasn't the only one under Miss Blue's spell in the classroom; most of us came away with that sort of full, silent feeling that you have after you've seen a really good movie and you have to walk back out into the real world again.

Who would have thought my shrivelled heart
Could have recovered greenness? It was gone
Quite underground as flowers depart
To see their mother-root when they have blown;
   Where they together
All the hard weather,
Dead to the world, keep house unknown.

These are thy wonders, Lord of Power
Killing and quickening, bringing down to hell
And up to heaven, in an hour;
Making a chiming of a passing bell
   We say amiss
   This or that is:
Thy word is all, if we could spell.

George Herbert

4
All the Hard Weather

Sometimes our hearts do shrivel, and we wonder if anything can ever green them again.

There once were two princesses. One of them was loving and giving, and whenever she spoke pearls and diamonds and other precious stones fell from her mouth. The other was selfish and nasty, and whenever she spoke out came toads and snakes and lizards.

We are, all of us, both princesses, and sometimes we wonder why we have so many more toad days than diamond days. It is hard to accept both princesses within ourselves, but until we recognize the thoughts and actions that cause the snakes and slimy creatures, we'll never recover the repentance and lovingness that will bring back the pearls.

Harriet, in Louise Fitzhugh's *Harriet the Spy*, was constantly writing in a notebook. It was the first day of school when she wrote the following:

JANIE GETS STRANGER EVERY YEAR. I THINK SHE *MIGHT* BLOW UP THE WORLD. BETH ELLEN ALWAYS LOOKS LIKE SHE MIGHT CRY. . . .

Carrie Andrews got off the bus. Harriet wrote:

CARRIE ANDREWS IS CONSIDERABLY FATTER THIS YEAR

Laura Peters got out of the station wagon bus, Harriet wrote:

AND LAURA PETERS IS THINNER AND UGLIER. I THINK SHE COULD USE SOME BRACES ON HER TEETH.

"Oh, boy," said Sport. They looked and there was Pinky Whitehead. Pinky was so pale, thin, and weak that he looked like a glass of milk, a tall thin glass of milk. Sport couldn't bear to look at him. Harriet turned away from habit, then looked back to see if he had changed. Then she wrote:

PINKY WHITEHEAD HAS NOT CHANGED. PINKY WHITEHEAD WILL NEVER CHANGE.

Harriet consulted her mental notes on Pinky. He lived on Eighty-eighth Street. He had a very beautiful mother, a father who worked on a magazine, and a baby sister three years old. Harriet wrote:

MY MOTHER IS ALWAYS SAYING PINKY WHITEHEAD'S WHOLE PROBLEM IS HIS MOTHER. I BETTER ASK HER WHAT THAT MEANS OR I'LL NEVER FIND OUT. DOES HIS MOTHER HATE HIM? IF I HAD HIM I'D HATE HIM. . . .

The kind of tag they played wasn't very complicated; in fact Harriet thought it was rather silly. The object seemed to be to run around in circles and get very tired; then whoever was "it" tried to knock everyone else's books out of their arms. They played and played.

All of Rachel's books were on the ground, and some of Harriet's. They began to pick them up to go back and join the others.

Suddenly Harriet screeched in horror, "Where is my notebook?" They all began looking around, but they couldn't find it anywhere. Harriet suddenly remembered that some things had been knocked down before they ran away from the others. She began to run back toward them. She ran and ran, yelling like a banshee the whole way.

When she got back to where they had started she saw the whole class—Beth Ellen, Pinky Whitehead, Carrie Andrews, Marion Hawthorne, Laura Peters, and The Boy with the Purple Socks—all sitting around a bench while Janie Gibbs read to them from the notebook.

Harriet descended upon them with a scream that was supposed to frighten Janie so much she would drop the book. But Janie didn't frighten easily. She just stopped reading and looked up calmly. The others looked up too. She looked at all their eyes and suddenly Harriet M. Welsch was afraid.

They just looked and looked, and their eyes were the meanest eyes she had ever seen. They formed a little knot and wouldn't let her near them. Rachel and Sport came up then. Marion Hawthorne said fiercely, "Rachel, come over here." Rachel walked over to her, and after Marion had whispered in her ear, got the same mean look.

Janie said, "Sport, come over here."

"Whadaya mean?" said Sport.

"I have something to tell you," Janie said in a very pointed way. . . .

Janie passed the notebook to Sport and Rachel, never taking her eyes off Harriet as she did so. "Sport, you're on page thirty-four; Rachel, you're on fifteen," she said quietly. . . .

"Read it aloud Sport," said Janie harshly.

"I can't." Sport hid his face.

The book was passed back to Janie. Janie read the passage in a solemn voice.

SOMETIMES I CAN'T STAND SPORT. WITH HIS WORRYING ALL THE TIME AND FUSSING OVER HIS FATHER, SOMETIMES HE'S LIKE A LITTLE OLD WOMAN.

Sport turned his back on Harriet, but even from his back Harriet could see that he was crying.

I ache for Harriet, because of my own memories of the times when I have hurt people, not wittingly, not deliberately setting out to cause hurt, but by carelessness, insensitivity. Our stories of failure can be as creative a part of our lives as our stories of success, and some of them can open our hearts.

One time at boarding school I hurt my roommate, simply by being too busy to understand how unhappy she was when she had a letter telling her that the boy she expected to take her to the school dance had chicken pox. As far as I was concerned, dances were painful and had to be endured, if someone arranged a date for me. The world of dances and coming-out parties was one in which I was uncomfortable. But it was of paramount importance to my friend. And when I heard that her date had chicken pox, I laughed.

And she cried.

And then I realized how thoughtless I had been.

But she quickly forgave me, and we made up.

When the rising bell rang the next morning she leaped out of bed first. "Good morning," she said.

And I knew that all was well with us. "Good morning," I replied gloomily, thinking of the algebra test which lay ahead. "If it is a good morning, which I doubt."

And then we laughed, because we had read A. A. Milne's *Winnie-the-Pooh* aloud, and we could retell it almost line by line.

We have our Eeyore days, as we have our pearl or toad days, but I hope I'll never forget Eeyore's total happiness as he put the deflated balloon in and out of the empty pot. And we've all felt the way Pooh and Piglet did, chagrined and foolish, when something we've planned for someone else just doesn't work out. I'm still a little embarrassed about a pink glass gravy boat which I bought at Bloomingdale's for my mother when I was nine or ten. I thought it was absolutely beautiful, and it was in extreme bad taste. But her graciousness redeemed it.

"You seem so sad, Eeyore."

"Sad? Why should I be sad? It's my birthday. The happiest day of the year."

"Your birthday?" said Pooh in great surprise.

"Of course it is. Can't you see? Look at all the presents I have had." He waved a foot from side to side. "Look at the birthday cake. Candles and pink sugar."

Pooh looked—first to the right and then to the left.

"Presents?" said Pooh. "Birthday cake?" said Pooh. *"Where?"*

"Can't you see them?"

"No," said Pooh.

"Neither can I," said Eeyore. "Joke," he explained. "Ha ha!"

Pooh scratched his head, being a little puzzled by all this.

"But is it really your birthday?" he asked.

"It is."

"Oh! Well, Many happy returns of the day, Eeyore."

"And many happy returns to you, Pooh Bear."

"But it isn't *my* birthday."

"No, it's mine."

"But you said 'Many happy returns'——"

"Well, why not? You don't always want to be miserable on my birthday, do you?"

"Oh, I see," said Pooh.

"It's bad enough," said Eeyore, almost breaking down, "being miserable myself, what with no presents and no cake and no candles, and no proper notice taken of me at all, but if everybody else is going to be miserable too——"

This was too much for Pooh. "Stay there!" he called to Eeyore, as he turned and hurried back home as quick as he could; for he felt that he must get poor Eeyore a present of *some* sort at once, and he could always think of a proper one afterwards.

Outside his house he found Piglet, jumping up and down trying to reach the knocker.

"Hallo, Piglet," he said.

"Hallo, Pooh," said Piglet.

"What are *you* trying to do?"

"I was trying to reach the knocker," said Piglet. . . .

"Let me do it for you," said Pooh kindly. So he reached up and knocked at the door. "I have just seen Eeyore," he began, "and poor Eeyore is in a Very Sad Condition, because it's his birthday, and nobody has taken any notice of it. . . .

"What a long time whoever lives here is answering this door." And he knocked again.

"But Pooh," said Piglet, "it's your own house!"

"Oh!" said Pooh. "So it is," he said. "Well, let's go in."

So in they went. The first thing Pooh did was to go to the cupboard to see if he had quite a small jar of honey left; and he had, so he took it down.

"I'm giving this to Eeyore," he explained, "as a present. What are *you* going to give?"

"Couldn't I give it too?" said Piglet. "From both of us?"

"No," said Pooh. "That would *not* be a good plan."

"All right, then, I'll give him a balloon. I've got one left from my party." . . .

"That, Piglet, is a *very* good idea. It is just what Eeyore wants to cheer him up. Nobody can be uncheered with a balloon."

So off Piglet trotted; and in the other direction went Pooh, with his jar of honey.

It was a warm day, and he had a long way to go. He hadn't gone more than half-way when a sort of funny feeling began to creep all over him. It began at the tip of his nose and trickled all through him and out at the soles of his feet. It was just as if somebody inside him were saying, "Now then, Pooh, time for a little something."

"Dear, dear," said Pooh, "I didn't know it was as late as that." So he sat down and took the top off his jar of honey. "Lucky I brought this with me," he thought. "Many a bear going out on a warm day like this would never have thought of bringing a little something with him." And he began to eat.

"Now let me see," he thought, as he took his last lick of the inside of the jar, "where was I going? Ah, yes, Eeyore." He got up slowly.

And then, suddenly, he remembered. He had eaten Eeyore's birthday present!

"Bother!" said Pooh. "What *shall* I do? I *must* give him *something*."

For a little while he couldn't think of anything. Then he thought: "Well, it's a very nice pot, even if there's no honey in it. . . . Eeyore could keep things in it, which might be Useful." . . .

While all this was happening, Piglet had gone back to his own house to get Eeyore's balloon. He held it very tightly against himself, so that it shouldn't blow away, and he ran as fast as he could so as to get to Eeyore before Pooh did; for he thought that he would like to be the first one to give a present, just as if he had thought of it without being told by anybody. And running along, and thinking how pleased Eeyore would be, he didn't look where he was going . . . and suddenly he put his foot in a rabbit hole, and fell down flat on his face.

BANG!!!???***!!!

Piglet lay there, wondering what had happened. . . .

"Well, that's funny," he thought. "I wonder what that bang was. I couldn't have made such a noise just falling down. And where's my balloon? And what's that small piece of damp rag doing?"

It was the balloon!

"Oh, dear!" said Piglet. "Oh, dear, oh, dearie, dearie, dear! Well, it's too late now. I can't go back, and I haven't another balloon, and perhaps Eeyore doesn't *like* balloons so *very* much."

So he trotted on, rather sadly now, and down he came to the side of the stream where Eeyore was, and called out to him.

"Good morning, Eeyore," shouted Piglet.

"Good morning, Little Piglet," said Eeyore. "If it *is* a good morning," he said. "Which I doubt," said he. "Not that it matters," he said.

"Many happy returns of the day," said Piglet, having now got closer.

Eeyore stopped looking at himself in the stream, and turned to stare at Piglet.

"Just say that again," he said. . . .

"Many happy returns of the day," said Piglet again.

"Meaning me?"

"Of course, Eeyore."

"My birthday?"

"Yes."

"Me having a real birthday?"

"Yes, Eeyore, and I've brought you a present." . . .

"Meaning me again?"

"Yes."

"My birthday still?"

"Of course, Eeyore."

"Me going on having a real birthday?"

"Yes, Eeyore, and I brought you a balloon."

"Balloon?" said Eeyore. "You did say balloon? One of those big coloured things you blow up? Gaiety, song-and-dance, here we are and there we are?"

"Yes, but I'm afraid—I'm very sorry, Eeyore—but when I was running along to bring it you, I fell down."

"Dear, dear, how unlucky! You ran too fast, I expect. You didn't hurt yourself, Little Piglet?"

"No, but I—I—oh, Eeyore, I burst the balloon!"

There was a very long silence.

"My balloon?" said Eeyore at last.

Piglet nodded.

"My birthday balloon?"

"Yes, Eeyore," said Piglet, sniffing a little. "Here it is. With—with many happy returns of the day." And he gave Eeyore the small piece of damp rag.

"Is this it?" said Eeyore, a little surprised.

Piglet nodded.

"My present?"

Piglet nodded again.

"The balloon?"

"Yes."

"Thank you, Piglet,"said Eeyore. "You don't mind my asking," he went on, "but what colour was this balloon when it—when it *was* a balloon?"

"Red."

"I just wondered. . . . Red," he murmured to himself. "My favourite colour. . . . How big was it?"

"About as big as me."

"I just wondered . . . About as big as Piglet," he said to himself sadly. "My favourite size. Well, well."

Piglet felt very miserable, and didn't know what to say. He was still opening his mouth to begin something, and then deciding that it wasn't any good saying *that,* when he heard a shout from the other side of the river, and thoro wao Pooh.

"Many happy returns of the day," called out Pooh, forgetting that he had said it already.

"Thank you, Pooh, I'm having them," said Eeyore gloomily.

"I've brought you a little present," said Pooh excitedly.

"I've had it," said Eeyore. . . .

"It's a Useful Pot," said Pooh. "Here it is. And it's got 'A Very Happy Birthday with love from Pooh' written on it. That's what all that writing is. And it's for putting things in. There!"

When Eeyore saw the pot, he became quite excited.

"Why!" he said. "I believe my Balloon will just go into that Pot!"

"Oh, no, Eeyore," said Pooh. "Balloons are much too big to go into Pots. What you do with a balloon is, you hold the balloon——"

"Not mine," said Eeyore proudly. "Look, Piglet!" And as Piglet looked sorrowfully round, Eeyore picked the balloon up with his teeth, and placed it carefully in the pot; picked it out and put it on the ground; and then picked it up again and put it carefully back.

"So it does!" said Pooh. "It goes in!"

"So it does!" said Piglet. "And it comes out!"

"Doesn't it?" said Eeyore. "It goes in and out like anything."

"I'm very glad," said Pooh happily, "that I thought of giving you a Useful Pot to put things in."

"I'm very glad," said Piglet happily, "that I thought of giving you Something to put in a Useful Pot."

But Eeyore wasn't listening. He was taking the balloon out, and putting it back again, as happy as could be.

The subject of punishment is a difficult one, because, somewhere along the line, punishment has become confused with revenge.

There is really only one purpose for punishment, and that is to teach a lesson, and there is only one lesson to be taught, and that is love. Otherwise it is not punishment, it is revenge or retribution.

This is the painful lesson Nat learns in Louisa May Alcott's *Little Men*. The lesson of love is the most difficult punishment of all, for it means that we have to realize what we have done, be truly sorry, and turn, humbly, to that love which is offered us.

Confusing punishment with revenge has further confounded us into confusing judgment with vindictiveness. Far too many people fear the Last Judgment because they believe God is really going to zotz them for all their wrongdoings, tearing off the few Brownie points they've acquired and trampling them in the dust.

Or, what is worse, they look forward to the Last Judgment because that is when God is really going to zotz all their enemies, and they, the saved, can rejoice in the torments of the damned in hell.

But if, as Emily Byrd Starr's father said, we can't help liking God, because God is Love itself, then pictures of judgment as revenge and vindictiveness simply do not work. Jesus points out that a human parent would not give a child a scorpion instead of an egg, and reminds his listeners that if human parents want good things for their children, how much more God wants good things for all of us.

One fault of Nat's gave the Bhaers much anxiety, although they saw how it had been strengthened by fear and ignorance. . . . Nat sometimes told lies.

"You cannot be too careful," . . . said Mr. Bhaer, in one of the talks he had with Nat about his chief temptation.

"I know it, and I don't mean to, but it's so much easier to get along if you ain't very fussy about being exactly true. I used to tell 'em because I was afraid of father and Nicolo, and now I do sometimes because the boys laugh at me. I know it's bad, but I forget," and Nat looked much depressed by his sins.

"When I was a little lad I used to tell lies! Ach! what fibs they were, and my old grandmother cured me of it—how, do you think? My parents had talked, and cried, and punished, but still did I forget as you. Then said the dear old grandmother, 'I shall help you to remember, and put a check on this unruly part,' with that she drew out my tongue and snipped the end with her scissors till the blood ran. That was terrible, you may believe, but it did me much good, because it was sore for days, and every word I said came so slowly that I had time to think. After that I was more careful, and got on better, for I feared the big scissors. Yet the dear grandmother was most kind to me in all things. . . .

"I never had any grandmothers, but if you think it will cure me, I'll let you snip my tongue," said Nat, heroically, for he dreaded pain. . . .

Mr. Bhaer smiled, but shook his head.

"I have a better way than that, I tried it once before and it worked well. See now, when you tell a lie I will not punish you, but you shall punish me."

"How?" asked Nat, startled at the idea.

"You shall ferule me in the good old-fashioned way, I seldom do it myself, but it may make you remember better to give me pain than to feel it yourself."

"Strike you? Oh, I couldn't!" cried Nat.

"Then mind that tripping tongue of thine. I have no wish to be hurt, but I would gladly bear much pain to cure this fault."

This suggestion made such an impression on Nat, that for a long time he set a watch upon his lips, and was desperately accurate, for Mr. Bhaer judged rightly, that love of him would be more powerful with Nat than fear for himself. But alas! one sad day Nat was off his guard, and when peppery Emil threatened to thrash him, if it was he who had run over his garden and broken down his best hills of corn, Nat declared he didn't, and then was ashamed to own up that he did do it, when Jack was chasing him the night before.

He thought no one would find it out, but Tommy happened to see him, and when Emil spoke of it a day or two later, Tommy gave his evidence, and Mr. Bhaer heard it. School was over, and they were all standing about in the hall, and Mr. Bhaer had just sat down on the straw settee, to enjoy his frolic with Teddy; but when he heard Tommy, and saw Nat turn scarlet, and look at him with a frightened face, he put the little boy down, saying, "Go to thy mother, bübchen,

I will come soon," and taking Nat by the hand led him into the school, and shut the door.

The boys looked at one another in silence for a minute, then Tommy slipped out and peeping in at the half-closed blinds, beheld a sight that quite bewildered him. Mr. Bhaer had just taken down the long rule that hung over his desk, so seldom used that it was covered with dust.

"My eye! he's going to come down heavy on Nat this time. Wish I hadn't told," thought good-natured Tommy, for to be feruled was the deepest disgrace at this school.

"You remember what I told you last time?" said Mr. Bhaer, sorrowfully, not angrily.

"Yes; but please don't make me, I can't bear it," cried Nat, backing up against the door with both hands behind him, and a face full of distress.

"I shall keep my word, and you must remember to tell the truth. Obey me, Nat, take this and give me six good strokes."

Tommy was so staggered by this last speech that he nearly tumbled down the bank, but saved himself, and hung on to the window ledge, staring in with eyes as round as the stuffed owl's on the chimney-piece.

Nat took the rule, for when Mr. Bhaer spoke in that tone every one obeyed him, and, looking as scared and guilty as if about to stab his master, he gave two feeble blows on the broad hand held out to him. Then he stopped and looked up, half blind with tears, but Mr. Bhaer said steadily,—

"Go on, and strike harder."

As if seeing that it must be done, and eager to have the hard task soon over, Nat drew his sleeve across his eyes and gave two more quick hard strokes that reddened the hand, yet hurt the giver more.

"Isn't that enough?" he asked in a breathless sort of tone.

"Two more," was all the answer, and he gave them, hardly seeing where they fell, then threw the rule all across the room, and hugging the kind hand in both his own, laid his face down on it sobbing out in a passion of love, and shame, and penitence.

I'm nobody, who are you?

Perhaps we have to be nobody before we can be somebody, anybody, everybody. It is one of God's greatest kindnesses to us that we do not see ourselves exactly as we are, because probably we couldn't bear to know how often we lie, as Nat did, hardly aware we're doing it; or how often we judge unkindly, as Harriet did, without meaning to hurt.

Conversely, it is a kindness to us that we don't know many of our beautiful qualities. Mister Beck did not know quite how much heaven he was giving in those garden squares; Caddie did not know how much love she was giving with the sale of her pony; Kenneth wasn't trying to be virtuous or score points when he offered to take the least desirable role in the Knights of the Round Table Game.

Admitting all this, we still have to come to terms with ourselves, accepting ourselves as we are, without one plea. When Dorothy, in L. Frank Baum's *The Wizard of Oz*, accuses the wizard of being a very bad man, he replies, "Oh, no, my dear; I'm really a very good man; but I'm a very bad wizard."

He was, in fact, the opposite kind of wizard from the wizard Ged was being taught to be, with reverence and humility. But, in acknowledging that he was a bad wizard, he was also learning something very important and teaching it to Dorothy.

The Lion thought it might be as well to frighten the Wizard, so he gave a large, loud roar, which was so fierce and dreadful that Toto jumped away from him in alarm and tipped over the screen that stood in a corner. As it fell with a crash they looked that way, and the next moment all of them were filled with wonder. For they saw, standing in just the spot the screen had hidden, a little, old man, with a bald head and a wrinkled face, who seemed to be as much surprised as they were. The Tin Woodman, raising his axe, rushed toward the little man and cried out,

"Who are you?"

"I am Oz, the Great and Terrible," said the little man, in a trembling voice, "but don't strike me—please don't!—and I'll do anything you want me to."

Our friends looked at him in surprise and dismay.

"I thought Oz was a great Head," said Dorothy.

"And I thought Oz was a lovely Lady," said the Scarecrow.

"And I thought Oz was a terrible Beast," said the Tin Woodman.

"And I thought Oz was a Ball of Fire," exclaimed the Lion.

"No; you are all wrong," said the little man, meekly. "I have been making believe."

"Making believe!" cried Dorothy. "Are you not a great Wizard?"

"Hush, my dear," he said; "don't speak so loud, or you will be overheard—and I should be ruined. I'm supposed to be a Great Wizard."

"And aren't you?" she asked.

"Not a bit of it, my dear; I'm just a common man."

"You're more than that," said the Scarecrow, in a grieved tone; "you're a humbug."

"Exactly so!" declared the little man, rubbing his hands together as if it pleased him; "I am a humbug."

Each year as I read the great stories of Scripture, it becomes more and more apparent to me that the people God chooses to do the work of the Kingdom are not chosen because they are worthy or virtuous or qualified or because they deserve to be chosen.

Joseph with his coat of many colors was a spoiled younger son of an indulgent father, justly infuriating his elder brothers with his bragging. But there was no question of whether or not Joseph was *worthy;* Joseph was *called.*

Jesus was not very tolerant with the smugly qualified. He didn't think much of the Pharisee who knew how well he kept the law and how good and charitable he was.

I don't have much trouble in separating myself from that Pharisee. Or do I? What happens when I read about Pauline, in Noel Streatfeild's *Ballet Shoes?*

In my early years in school, particularly the middle years, fourth through seventh grades, I was anything but a success. My teachers thought I was stupid. My classmates knew I'd lose the relay races for them. I was the last one to be chosen for anything.

So, when I got to high school, and my teachers appreciated me, and my classmates liked me, I was happy indeed.

In the spring of my junior year, elections were held for the President of Student Council for the following year. I was one of those up for election, and I wanted to win, oh, how I wanted to win.

It became apparent that the choice was going to be between me and one other girl. When things trouble or confuse me, I often try to work it out in verse. I wanted to win this election. I wanted God to let me win. But I knew that the other girl, who would not, I was certain, make a good president, also wanted to win.

I remember the last two lines of the poem I wrote about this:

> We both want this in every way.
> Can it be right for us to pray?

The other girl won the election. I didn't think she was as qualified to run the student government as I was. I didn't think she cared about the school as much as I did. I felt terrible.

Maybe I lost the election because I was being like the Pharisee. I went home and took a fresh look at myself, and my head, which had been rather swollen, went down to normal size.

When I got back to school in September, the girl who had won the election had not returned. There was another election, and I was elected. And I was a far better president of student government than I would have been had I won the election the year before, when I thought it was a matter of winning, and qualification, and popularity. It was a responsibility, and a heavy one. But, oh, Pauline, we are sisters, you and I.

Pauline was a great success as "Alice." All the papers said so, and published photographs of her. The children who came to see the play wrote her letters and sent her chocolates, and told her she was wonderful, and the grown-ups in the cast were nice to her, and she could not help seeing that they thought she was good. The result was she became very conceited. Petrova and Posy [her adopted sisters] were the first to bear the brunt of it. Pauline thought because she was the leading lady in the theater she was one in the house too, and of course they were not standing for that. It began with her telling them to fetch things for her, and to pick things up she had dropped. Posy, being good-natured, and not very noticing, did what she asked once or twice. Then Petrova said:

"Has something happened to your legs and arms?"

" 'Course not," Pauline answered. "Why?"

Petrova raised her eyebrows.

"I would have thought a person whose arms and legs were all right would have been able to fetch their own pocket handkerchief, and pick up their own wool."

Pauline flushed.

"Why shouldn't Posy? I get used to people doing things for me in the theater."

Posy looked at Petrova, then they both looked at Pauline.

"It's going to be difficult," Petrova said thoughtfully, "when we are all working, isn't it, Posy?"

Posy nodded.

"All of us being like Queens at once."

Pauline got up.

"I think you're both being hateful." She slammed the door.

As the run of the play went on, Pauline got worse. She was very nice on the stage, because everybody was nice to her, but she was very different at home, and in her dressing-room. She had a dressing-room to herself, but it was arranged that Winifred [her under-study] should sit in it, . . .

As an under-study she was allowed to leave the theater as soon as Pauline had gone on for the last act; but she had a dull job, especially for somebody as clever as she was, who could have played the part beautifully herself. It was difficult for her not to be jealous, with Pauline having all the fun, flowers, chocolates, letters, and praise; but she managed to pretend she did not mind, and spent all her afternoons knitting a jersey, and talking to Nana. Nana understood just how she must feel, and was very nice to her; but Pauline, getting more conceited every day, stopped being sorry for her, and bragged instead about what people had said, and all the presents she got, and even expected Winifred to fetch and carry for her. Nana was shocked that anybody she had brought up could behave so atrociously. . . .

The rule of the theater was that a cotton wrap had to be worn over all stage dresses until just before an entrance. Nana always saw that Pauline's wrap was round her when she went on to the side of the stage, and she hung it up for her when she made her entrance. When Pauline came off after the act, or during an act, she was supposed to wrap it round her. To start with Pauline was very good at remembering it, but after a bit she thought it a bore and left it hanging where Nana had left it, and the call-boy had to bring it to her dressing-room. This went on for a day or two; then one afternoon Pauline was skipping off after the first act, when the stage manager caught hold of her.

"What about your wrap, my dear?"

"Oh, bother!" said Pauline. "Tell the call-boy to bring it." And she ran to her room.

The stage manager took the wrap and followed her; he knocked on her door. Nana opened it.

"Good afternoon, Miss Gutheridge. Pauline must remember her wrap. The call-boy has other things to do than to run after her, and it is a rule of the management's that she wear it."

Nana called Pauline.

"Why did you leave your wrap on the stage?"

"Why shouldn't I?" Pauline said grandly. "Stupid things, anyway."

The stage manager looked at her in surprise, as up till then he had thought her a nice child.

"Stupid or not, you're to wear it."

He went back to the stage.

For two or three days Pauline wore her wrap; then one afternoon she deliberately left it on the stage after the last act. A few minutes later the call-boy knocked on her door.

"Mr. Barnes's compliments, Miss Fossil, and will you go back for your wrap."

"Tell him 'No'," Pauline shouted. "I'm busy." . . .

After a few minutes there was another knock on the door. This time it was Mr. Barnes.

"Did Pauline get my message?" he asked Nana.

Pauline pushed Nana to one side and came out into the passage.

"I did, and I said I wouldn't fetch it, so please stop bothering."

Mr. French, who was the managing director of the Princess Theatres, Ltd., came out of the "Mad Hatter's" dressing-room, which was next door. He stopped in surprise.

"What's all the trouble?"

Mr. Barnes looked worried, as he hated telling tales. But Nana thought a scolding would be the best thing in the world for Pauline. She told him the whole story. Mr. French looked down at Pauline.

"Go and fetch your wrap at once. I don't make rules in my theater for little girls to break."

Pauline was excited and angry, and she completely lost her temper. She behaved as she had never behaved before. She stamped her foot.

"Get it yourselves if you want it fetched."

There was a long pause, and in the silence Pauline began to feel frightened. Mr. French was a terribly important man, and nobody was ever rude to him. His face expressed nothing, but she could feel he was angry. At last he looked at Mr. Barnes.

"Is the under-study in the theater?"

Nana called Winifred, who came out looking very nervous, for she had heard all that had gone on.

"You will play tomorrow," Mr. French said to her. "Pauline will be in the theater as your under-study."

He went down the passage and never gave Pauline another look.

Pauline finished taking off her make-up, and got dressed, and went home in perfect silence; her mouth was pressed together. Winifred thought it was because she was angry, but Nana knew it was not. She knew that Pauline was terrified to speak in case she should break down and cry. . . . As soon as she got into the house she raced up the stairs. She could not go into the bedroom, because the others might come in, so she went into the bathroom and locked the door, and lay down on the floor, just as she was, in a coat, gloves, and beret, and cried dreadfully. At first she cried because she thought she was being badly treated, and kept muttering, "It's a shame; I didn't do anything." "Anyhow, Winifred's sure to be awful; they'll be sorry." But by degrees, as she got more and more tired from crying, other thoughts drifted through her mind. Had she been rude? Had she been showing off? Inside she knew that she had, and she was ashamed, and though she was quite alone she turned red.

As soon as the other three had gone downstairs, Nana knocked on the bathroom door, and told Pauline to let her in. Pauline lay where she was for a few minutes, too tired and too miserable and too ashamed to come out; then she turned the key. Nana put her arm round her.

"Come along," she said, "you'll feel better after a bath and something to eat." . . .

She treated Pauline just as if she were six instead of twelve, helping her off with her clothes, and even washing bits of her, then she put her in the armchair by the fire and gave her a large bowl of bread and milk.

"You eat all that, dear, and stop fretting. Pride has to come before a fall, and that's the law of nature; you've got your fall, and now you've got to be brave and get up again. What's one matinée, anyhow, and if you think right, you'll be glad in a way that poor Winifred gets a chance one afternoon. She's been very good, knitting quietly." Nana gave her a kiss. . . .

At the matinée the next day she took a bit of sewing to do, and sat quietly in a corner working. She wished Winifred luck before she went on, and when she heard the "Mad Hatter" congratulating her in the passage outside, she managed to smile, and tell her she was glad, though inside she was not really, as of course she hoped nobody was as good an "Alice" as herself. Just as the last act started, Mr. Barnes came to the door and called her. He was nice; he told her Mr. French wanted to see her, and that though Winifred was very good, they'd all missed her, and would be glad to see her back tomorrow.

Mr. French had a large office, where Pauline had never been before. He was sitting writing at a desk. He told Pauline to sit. Instead she came over to the desk and said politely that she was sorry she had been rude and disobedient yesterday, and that she would not be again. He said that was quite all right; she had done very nicely as "Alice," and that doing nicely in a part always went to an actress's head to begin with. It was a good thing to get that sort of thing over at twelve, instead of waiting till she was grown-up. He then said that Winifred had done very nicely as "Alice" too, and that she might take note of it, because it was an object lesson she might remember always. That nobody was irreplaceable. . . .

Pauline went to sleep [that night] feeling terribly glad the day was over and she would be "Alice" again tomorrow, and, down inside, rather surprised to find how right Mr. French was. It really would not matter terribly if she was ill, and Winifred played for the rest of the run. She pushed the thought back, but she knew it was true.

Pauline was responsible for her own behavior. Success went to her head, and so she lost her head and found it again.

But sometimes things happen without our intention; a small action snowballs into something enormous. When David Lurie in Chaim Potok's *In the Beginning* hit the dog, he had not any idea that this action would lead to the dog's death. And perhaps he was as much confused at the variety of reactions to what happened as he was grieved.

Sooner or later we experience something similar to Potok's story of the accidental causing of a dog's death. Once I watched a scuffle in the classroom; it became rougher than intended, and the point of a pencil accidentally went into one ten-year-old's eye. And the eye was lost. It didn't happen to me, but it could have. There was no ambiguity in the reactions here; nobody said it didn't matter, or that it was for the best. But the child who caused it had to live with the blinding of an eye for the rest of his life.

Sometimes the accidental wrongdoings are as difficult for us to accept as those we are, ourselves, responsible for. And then, of course, there's Pooh and Piglet and the honey jar and the broken balloon!

But God forgives us as long as we turn and say, from the depths of our hearts, "I didn't mean to be careless." "I never meant anybody to be hurt." "I'm sorry I was self-centered and prideful."

We all have something to live with, something we have done which makes us ashamed. Sometimes I am better able to accept God's forgiveness of my unloving actions than my own forgiveness of myself. But until we accept whatever it is we have done and are forgiven, we cannot move on in the continuing process of growing up.

I liked things to be quiet. I did not even like it when our new canary sang too long. But I did not open my window to let our first canary fly out. I would not do anything like that. It had really been an accident.

Like the accident with the dog. . . .

My father came home early from his office one day and saw me with the dog. He shooed the dog away with his Yiddish newspaper and said to me, "Dogs are dirty."

I hung my head. It was two or three weeks after the canary had flown out of my window.

"In Europe dogs were trained by the goyim to bite Jews. I detest dogs. Keep that filthy dog away from the carriage. Do you hear?"

"Yes, Papa."

"And do not put your hands in your mouth or your eyes until you wash them."

"Yes, Papa."

"And do not look so unhappy. It is not the end of the world."

He peered into the carriage, smiled briefly at my sleeping brother, and went into our apartment house. The dog sniffed at a tree near the edge of the sidewalk and went off to join a crowd of kids playing with bottle caps near Mr. Steinberg's candy store. . . .

The next day I saw the dog urinating on one of the wheels of my brother's carriage. Then he got up on his hind legs and stood there, his forelegs on the carriage, his head poking around inside, his tail wagging. I had moved away from the carriage to join a game of marbles. I rushed back and with my open hand—my father had smacked me that way when the canary had gone through my open window—hit the dog hard on his hindquarters above the wagging tail and shouted, "Go away!" The dog yelped, ran into the street, and was struck by a car.

The front left wheel of the car ran over his head. The rear wheel ran over his back. The car braked to a stop. All up and down the block everyone froze. Heads turned. The dog let out short, ear-piercing, yelping cries. . . .

I leaned against his carriage, cold and trembling, my legs barely able to support my body. Mrs. Horowitz came rushing out of our apartment house. . . . She looked at Shaigitz and screamed.

I leaned forward away from my brother's carriage and vomited my breakfast onto the sidewalk. My nose began to bleed.

"It was an accident," I kept saying, holding a handkerchief to my nose.

"What did you hit him for?" the kids on the block kept saying.

"He had his head right in the carriage," I kept saying.

"You could have told him to go away," they kept saying. "What did you hit him for?"

"It was an accident," I said to my father.

"Do not worry yourself over it. He was a filthy dog. Who needed him around making dirt on the sidewalk and overturning the garbage cans? Do not look so sad. It is not the end of the world."

"It was an accident," I said to my mother.

She blinked her eyes nervously. "In Europe they made less fuss when a Jew was killed than they are making over this dog."

"I thought he would bite Alex."

"Of course," my mother said. "Why else would you have hit him like that?"

"It was an accident," I said to my cousin.

"Sure," he said, and gave me a pitying look which I did not understand and was afraid to ask him to explain.

"You killed my dog!" Mrs. Horowitz screamed at me one afternoon in the entrance hall of our apartment house. "I'm all alone!"

"It was an accident," I cried.

O World, thou choosest not the better part!
It is not wisdom to be only wise
And on the inward vision close the eyes,
But it is wisdom to believe the heart.
Columbus found a world, and had no chart,
Save one that faith deciphered in the skies;
To trust the soul's invincible surmise
Was all his science and his only art.
Our knowledge is a torch of smoky pine,
That lights the pathway but one step ahead
Across a void of mystery and dread.
Bid, then, the tender light of faith to shine
By which alone the mortal heart is led
Unto the thinking of the thought divine.

George Santayana

5

It Is Wisdom
to Believe the Heart

Mark Twain's *The Adventures of Tom Sawyer* was a book I read not once but many times. It is such fun! But the following story always bothered me. Why did it remind me of the time when I couldn't have been more then five or six and went to a birthday party? One of the games was "pin the tail on the donkey," and after my eyes had been bandaged I could see just a tiny bit, just enough so that I pinned the tail closest to the right place on the donkey.

The prize was something I'd always wanted.

But I never liked it.

The things that hurt us which come from outside ourselves usually hurt us less than those we ourselves have caused.

Tom, Huck Finn, and Joe Harper ran away from home. They got as far as an island several miles from their village and set up camp. The story is told here in abridged form.

They came back to camp wonderfully refreshed, glad-hearted, and ravenous; and they soon had the camp-fire blazing up again. Huck found a spring of clear cold water close by, and the boys made cups of broad oak or hickory leaves. While Joe was slicing bacon for breakfast, Tom and Huck asked him to hold on a minute; they stepped to a promising nook in the river-bank and threw in their lines; almost immediately they had reward. They fried the fish with the bacon, and were astonished; for no fish had ever seemed so delicious before.

They then went off through the woods on an exploring expedition. They tramped gaily along, over decaying logs, through tangled underbrush, among solemn monarchs of the forest, hung from their crowns to the ground with a drooping regalia of grapevines. Now and then they came upon snug nooks carpeted with grass and jeweled with flowers

It was close upon the middle of the afternoon when they got back to camp. They fared sumptuously upon cold ham, and then threw themselves down in the shade to talk. But the talk soon began to drag. The stillness, the solemnity that brooded in the woods, and the sense of loneliness, began to tell upon the spirits of the boys. A sort of undefined longing crept upon them.

For some time, now, the boys had been dully conscious of a peculiar sound in the distance. But now this mysterious sound became more pronounced, and forced a recognition. The boys started, glanced at each other, and then each assumed a listening attitude. There was a long silence, profound and unbroken; then a deep, sullen boom came floating down out of the distance.

"What is it!" exclaimed Joe, under his breath.

They parted the bushes on the bank and peered out over the water. The little steam ferryboat was about a mile below the village, drifting with the current. Her broad deck seemed crowded with people. Presently a great jet of white smoke burst from the ferryboat's side, and as it expanded and rose in a lazy cloud, that same dull throb of sound was borne to the listeners again.

"I know now!" exclaimed Tom; "somebody's drownded!"

"That's it!" said Huck; "they done that last summer, when Bill Turner got drownded; they shoot a cannon over the water, and that makes him come up to the top."

"By jings, I wish I was over there, now," said Joe.

"I do too," said Huck. "I'd give heaps to know who it is."

The boys still listened and watched. Presently a revealing thought flashed through Tom's mind, and he exclaimed:

"Boys, I know who's drownded—it's us!"

They felt like heroes in an instant. Here was a gorgeous triumph; they were missed; they were mourned; hearts were breaking on their account; tears were being shed; accusing memories of unkindnesses to these poor lost lads were rising up, and unavailing regrets and remorse were being indulged: and best of all, the departed were the talk of the whole town.

But when the shadows of night closed them in, they gradually ceased to talk, and sat gazing into the fire, with their minds evidently wandering elsewhere. The excitement was gone, now, and Tom and Joe could not keep back thoughts of certain persons at home who were not enjoying this fine frolic as much as they were.

[Thoughts of home and a mourning Aunt Polly overcame Tom. Under the cover of the darkness he swam ashore.]

He flew along unfrequented alleys, and shortly found himself at his aunt's back fence. He climbed over and looked in at the sitting-room window. There sat Aunt Polly, Sid, Mary, and Joe Harper's mother, grouped together, talking. They were by the bed, and the bed was between them and the door. Tom went to the door and began to softly lift the latch; then he pressed gently, and the door yielded a crack; he continued pushing cautiously, and quaking every time it creaked, till he judged he might squeeze through on his knees. He lay hidden under the bed.

"But as I was saying," said Aunt Polly, "he warn't *bad,* so to say— only misch*ee*vous. Only just giddy, and harum-scarum, you know. He warn't any more responsible than a colt. *He* never meant any harm, and he was the best-hearted boy that ever was"—and she began to cry.

"It was just so with my Joe—always full of his devilment, and up to every kind of mischief, but he was just as unselfish and kind as he could be." Mrs. Harper sobbed as if her heart would break.

"Oh, Mrs. Harper, I don't know how to give him up! I don't know how to give him up! He was such a comfort to me, although he tormented my old heart out of me, 'most."

"The Lord giveth and the Lord hath taken away,—blessed be the name of the Lord! But it's *so* hard—oh, it's so hard! Only last Saturday my Joe busted a firecracker right under my nose and I knocked him sprawling. Little did I know then how soon—Oh, if it was to do over again I'd hug him and bless him for it."

Tom went on listening. It was believed that the search for the bodies had been a fruitless effort merely because the drowning must have occurred in mid-channel. If the bodies continued missing until Sunday, all hope would be given over, and the funerals would be preached on that morning. Tom shuddered.

Mrs. Harper gave a sobbing good night and turned to go. Then with a mutual impulse the two women flung themselves into each other's arms and had a good, consoling cry, and then parted. Aunt Polly was very tender in her good night to Sid and Mary. Sid snuffled a bit and Mary went off crying with all her heart.

Aunt Polly knelt down and prayed for Tom so touchingly, so appealingly, and with such measureless love in her words and her old trembling voice, that he was weltering in tears again long before she was through.

He had to keep still long after she went to bed, for she kept making broken-hearted ejaculations from time to time and tossing unrestfully. But at last she was still, only moaning a little in her sleep. Now the boy stole out, shaded the candlelight with his hand, and stood regarding her. He bent over and kissed the faded lips, and straightway made his stealthy exit, latching the door behind him.

On Sunday the bell tolled, instead of ringing in the usual way. It was a very still Sabbath, and the mournful sound seemed in keeping. The villagers began to gather, loitering a moment in the vestibule to converse in whispers about the sad event. But there was no whispering in the house; only the funereal rustling of dresses as the women gathered to their seats disturbed the silence there. None could remember when the little church had been so full before. There was finally a waiting pause, an expectant dumbness, and then Aunt Polly entered, followed by Sid and Mary, and they by the Harper family, all in deep black, and the whole congregation, the old minister as well, rose reverently and stood, until the mourners were seated in the front pew. There was another communing silence, broken at intervals by muffled sobs, and then the minister spread his hands abroad and prayed. A moving hymn was sung, and the text followed: "I am the Resurrection and the Life."

As the service proceeded, the clergyman drew such pictures of the graces, the winning ways, and the rare promise of the lost lads, that every soul there, thinking he recognized these pictures, felt a pang in remembering that he had persistently blinded himself to them always before, and had as persistently seen only faults and flaws in the poor boys. The minister related many a touching incident in the lives of the departed, too, which illustrated their sweet, generous natures. The congregation became more and more moved, as the pathetic tale went on, till at last the whole company broke down and joined the weeping mourners in a chorus of anguished sobs, the preacher himself giving way to his feelings, and crying in the pulpit.

There was a rustle in the gallery, which nobody noticed; a moment later the church door creaked; the minister raised his streaming eyes above his handkerchief, and stood transfixed! First one and then another pair of eyes followed the minister's, and then almost with one impulse the congregation rose and stared while the three dead boys came marching up the aisle, Tom in the lead, Joe next, and Huck, a ruin of drooping rags, sneaking sheepishly in the rear! They had been hid in the unused gallery listening to their own funeral sermon!

Aunt Polly, Mary, and the Harpers threw themselves upon their restored ones, smothered them with kisses and poured out thanksgivings, while poor Huck stood abashed and uncomfortable, not knowing exactly what to do or where to hide from so many unwelcoming eyes. He wavered, and started to slink away, but Tom seized him and said:

"Aunt Polly, it ain't fair. Somebody's got to be glad to see Huck."

"And so they shall. *I'm* glad to see him, poor motherless thing!" And the loving attentions Aunt Polly lavished upon him were the one thing capable of making him more uncomfortable than he was before.

Suddenly the minister shouted at the top of his voice: "Praise God from whom all blessings flow—SING!—and put your hearts in it!"

And they did. Old Hundred swelled up with a triumphant burst, and while it shook the rafters Tom Sawyer looked around him and confessed in his heart that this was the proudest moment of his life.

As the "sold" congregation trooped out they said they would almost be willing to be made ridiculous again to hear Old Hundred sung like that once more.

Once upon a time when I was a child I was in Avignon, that ancient town of popes and the old nursery song, "Sur le pont d'Avignon, on y danse, on y danse." I stood on the bridge and looked down on the water flowing below, and although nobody was dancing, I skipped all the way across.

My father gave me twenty-five centimes, about five cents, for a slot machine in the lobby of the restaurant where my parents were having tea—probably to amuse me and get me out of the way so they could have their afternoon tea quietly. I put my coin in one of the slot machines, and I couldn't lose; money kept pouring out at me, and after a while I realized that the machine must be broken. So I went to another slot machine and lost all the money I had illegally won—except the original twenty-five centimes, which I kept. Gambling is obviously not a compulsion for me!

In *The Old Curiosity Shop*, Charles Dickens's description of the grandfather's inability to keep from gambling is a graphic description of compulsive behavior. There are many compulsions; alcohol is another example. But there are subtler ones. Cleanliness, for example, taken to an extreme with constant washing of hands, is a compulsion. Those who would burn books because they don't measure up to a small group's standard of Christianity are acting under compulsion, rather than reason or love. A compulsion is usually an excuse to help keep us from facing whatever it is we really ought to be doing.

It had been gradually getting overcast, and now the sky was dark and lowering. . . . Large drops of rain soon began to fall, and, as the storm clouds came sailing onward, others supplied the void they left behind and spread over all the sky. Then was heard the low rumbling of distant thunder, then the lightning quivered, and then the darkness of an hour seemed to have gathered in an instant.

Fearful of taking shelter beneath a tree or hedge, the old man and the child hurried along the high road, hoping to find some house in which they could seek a refuge from the storm, which had now burst forth in earnest, and every moment increased in violence. Drenched with the pelting rain, confused by the deafening thunder, and bewildered by the glare of the forked lightning, they would have passed a solitary house without being aware of its vicinity, had not a man, who was standing at the door, called lustily to them to enter.

"Your ears ought to be better than other folks' at any rate, if you make so little of the chance of being struck blind," he said, retreating from the door and shading his eyes with his hands as the jagged lightning came again. "What were you going past for, eh?" he added, as he closed the door and led the way along a passage to a room behind.

"We didn't see the house, sir, till we heard you calling," Nell replied.

"No wonder," said the man, "with this lightning in one's eyes, by-the-by. You had better stand by the fire here, and dry yourselves a bit.

The night being warm, there was a large screen drawn across the room, for a barrier against the heat of the fire. [Voices could be heard on the other side.]

"Nell, they're—they're playing cards," whispered the old man, suddenly interested. "Don't you hear them?"

"Look sharp with that candle," said the voice; "it's as much as I can do to see the pips on the cards as it is; and get this shutter closed as quick as you can, will you? Your beer will be the worse for tonight's thunder I expect.—Game! Seven-and-sixpence to me, old Isaac. Hand over."

"Do you hear, Nell, do you hear them?" whispered the old man again, with increased earnestness, as the money chinked upon the table.

The child saw with astonishment and alarm that his whole appearance had undergone a complete change. His face was flushed and eager, his eyes were strained, his teeth set, his breath came short and thick, and the hand he laid upon her arm trembled so violently that she shook beneath its grasp.

"Bear witness," he muttered, looking upward, "that I always said it; that I knew it, dreamed of it, felt it was the truth, and that it must be so! What money have we, Nell? Come! I saw you with money yesterday. What money have we? Give it to me."

"No, no, let me keep it, grandfather," said the frightened child. "Let us go away from here. Do not mind the rain. Pray let us go."

"Give it to me, I say," returned the old man fiercely. "Hush, hush, don't cry, Nell. If I spoke sharply, dear, I didn't mean it. It's for thy good. I have wronged thee, Nell, but I will right thee yet, I will indeed. Where is the money?"

"Do not take it," said the child. "Pray do not take it, dear. For both our sakes let me keep it, or let me throw it away—better let me throw it away, than you take it now. Let us go; do let us go."

"Give me the money," returned the old man, "I must have it. There—there—that's my dear Nell. I'll right thee one day, child, I'll right thee, never fear!"

She took from her pocket a little purse. He seized it with the same rapid impatience which had characterised his speech, and hastily made his way to the other side of the screen. It was impossible to restrain him, and the trembling child followed close behind.

"Now old gentleman," said Isaac, looking round. "Do you know either of us? This side of the screen is private, sir."

"I had no intention to offend," said the old man, looking anxiously at the cards. "I thought that—"

... "Who knows," said Isaac, with a cunning look, "but the gentleman may have civilly meant to ask if he might have the honour to take a hand with us!"

"I did mean it," cried the old man. "That is what I mean. That is what I want now!"

"I thought so," returned the same man. "Then who knows but the gentleman, anticipating our objection to play for love, civilly desired to play for money?"

The old man replied by shaking the little purse in his eager hand, and then throwing it down upon the table, and gathering up the cards as a miser would clutch at gold. . . .

"Is this the gentleman's little purse? A very pretty little purse. Rather a light purse," added Isaac, throwing it into the air and catching it dexterously, "but enough to amuse a gentleman for half an hour or so."

The child, in a perfect agony, drew her grandfather aside, and implored him, even then, to come away.

"Come; and we may be so happy," said the child.

"We *will* be happy," replied the old man hastily. "Let me go, Nell. The means of happiness are on the cards and the dice. We must rise from little winnings to great. There's little to be won here; but great will come in time. I shall but win back my own, and it's all for thee, my darling."

As he spoke he drew a chair to the table; and the other three closing round it at the same time, the game commenced.

The child sat by, and watched its progress with a troubled mind. Regardless of the run of luck, and mindful only of the desperate passion which had its hold upon her grandfather, losses and gains were to her alike.

The storm had raged for full three hours; the lightning had grown fainter and less frequent; the thunder, from seeming to roll and break above their heads, had gradually died away into a deep hoarse distance; and still the game went on, and still the anxious child was quite forgotten. [But at last the play came to an end and Isaac List rose the only winner.]

Nell's little purse was exhausted; but although it lay empty by his side, and the other players had now risen from the table, the old man sat poring over the cards, dealing them as they had been dealt before, and turning up the different hands to see what each man would have held if they had still been playing. He was quite absorbed in this occupation, when the child drew near and laid her hand upon his shoulder, telling him it was near midnight.

"See the curse of poverty, Nell," he said, pointing to the packs he had spread out upon the table. "If I could have gone on a little longer, only a little longer, the luck would have turned on my side. Yes, it's as plain as the marks upon the cards. See here—and there—and here again."

"Put them away," urged the child. "Try to forget them."

"Try to forget them!" he rejoined, raising his haggard face to hers, and regarding her with an incredulous stare. "To forget them! How are we ever to grow rich if I forget them?"

Somewhere, on some planet in some galaxy, there may be a perfect society. But nobody has ever written about a perfect society convincingly. They sound unreal and dull.

Just as there's no perfect society on this planet, there's no such thing as a perfect family, as Judy Blume shows so convincingly in *It's Not the End of the World.* We all let each other down. Parents, with the best will in the world, hurt their children, and children hurt their parents. And each other.

Once when I was speaking at a state librarians' meeting, I was asked, "What did you and Hugh do that was best for your children?" Without stopping to think, I replied, "We love each other." I'm sure that was right, that loving each other is the best possible thing we could have done for our children.

And when the love of parents is so shattered that divorce is inevitable, children have to learn to live with it, as they have to learn to live with other kinds of death.

Perhaps one of the hardest lessons to learn about any kind of death is that it need not destroy our faith in life, life given us by God. Jesus was always concerned about broken things, gathering up all the crumbs of bread after the feeding of the five thousand, healing broken people.

It may be easier for a child than an adult to understand that God is part of the death of a grandparent, and that death is not the end. It is more difficult in the death of a friendship or a marriage, but God is here, waiting to pick up the pieces with us.

Now that the police business is out of the way, they can have a chance to be alone, I thought. They'll see that they belong together. That we're a family. Any minute now Daddy will tell her he's sorry he left.

I stayed in the kitchen with Aunt Ruth and Uncle Dan. I guess they wanted to hear what was going to happen as much as I did.

The first thing Daddy said was, "I want the truth and I want it now."

"I have nothing to say to you," Mom told him.

"You damn well better have something to say! Because I want to know why my son ran away!"

"Your son!" Mom shouted. "He's my son too . . . and don't you forget it!"

"When I left this house he was fine," Daddy said. "But you fixed that, didn't you? . . .

"Now you listen to me," Daddy shouted.

"No!" Mom hollered. "I'm tired of listening to you."

"And I'm tired of the whole business. You don't know what you want. You never did. And you never will! Because you never grew up! You're still Ruth's baby!"

Aunt Ruth pressed her lips together so tight they disappeared.

My mother shouted, "I should have listened to Ruth a long time ago. I should have listened the first time I brought you home. She saw you for what you are. Conceited, selfish—"

"One more word and I'm going to take the kids away from you!"

"Don't you dare threaten me!" Mom screamed.

"I mean it. So help me. I'll have you declared incompetent."

"You rotten bastard . . ."

There was an awful crash in the living room then and I ran in to see what happened. One of Mom's best china babies was on the floor, smashed, like the mocha-icing cake.

"That's how you settle all your problems, isn't it?" Daddy said with a terrible laugh. "Just like a two-year-old."

Mom started to cry. She bent down and tried to pick up the pieces of her antique. I think it was the first time she ever broke anything she loved.

Sweet chance, that led my steps abroad
Beyond the town where wild flowers grow—
A rainbow and a cuckoo, Lord!
How rich and great the times are now!
Know, all ye sheep
And cows that keep
On staring that I stand so long
In grass that's wet from heavy rain—
A rainbow and a cuckoo's song
May never come together again;
May never come
This side the tomb.

W. H. Davies

6

A Rainbow
and a Cuckoo

The rainbow and the cuckoo, coming simultaneously, are part of that sense of wonder which makes us human.

"Oh, wonderful, wonderful, and most wonderful and yet again wonderful, and after that out of all whooping," cries Shakespeare's delighted and uninhibited Celia. Abraham Joshua Heschel felt that the loss of a sense of wonder is one of the most disastrous things to have happened in the twentieth century.

For the past six months I've been watching three golden retriever puppies almost visibly growing. They now have long adolescent legs and paws that are still too big for them, and they are hurtling golden balls of ecstatic love, and they are the sudden gentleness of a soft lick of the tongue, and they offer us utter trust as their ecstatic play stops suddenly and they fall into sleep.

The psalmist sings, "The heavens declare the glory of God; and the firmament showeth his handiwork." So full of wonder is the psalmist that in another song he sings, "The little hills shall rejoice on every side. The folds shall be full of sheep; the valleys also shall stand so thick with corn, that they shall laugh and sing."

In Antoine de Saint-Exupéry's *The Little Prince,* the prince, who came to earth from another planet, is talking to his friend on earth.

"The men where you live," said the little prince, "raise five thousand roses in the same garden—and they do not find in it what they are looking for."

"They do not find it," I replied.

"And yet what they are looking for could be found in one single rose, or in a little water."

"Yes, that is true," I said.

And the little prince added:

"But the eyes are blind. One must look with the heart."

I have a white china Buddha sitting on my desk, given me by
friends now dead. This Buddha has a look of loving forbearance,
and when things are out of sorts, or when I think I have cause to
be sorry for myself, this Buddha seems to say, "Oh, come on,
Madeleine, is it really as bad as all that? Put it in perspective. This,
too, shall pass. Come along, pick yourself up and get on with it." At
times when this is the kind of thing I need to hear, the Buddha is
a better Christ figure for me than a crucifix.

I do not worship the white china of the Buddha. If it were
accidentally broken it would not shake my faith. But it is a useful
symbol for me. So, sometimes, is hearty, loving, delighted laughter,
for so, I think, must Jesus have laughed, perhaps in that house in
Bethany where he was so welcome and so at home.

In Kenneth Grahame's *The Wind in the Willows*, when Mole and
Rat had the numinous experience of their vision of the Great God
Pan, that opened the gates of another heaven for me, too. And
surely Christ was there.

Fastening their boat to a willow, [Rat and Mole] landed in this
silent, silver kingdom, and patiently explored the hedges, the hollow
trees, the tunnels and their little culverts, the ditches and dry
waterways. Embarking again and crossing over, they worked their
way up the stream in this manner, while the moon, serene and
detached in a cloudless sky, did what she could, though so far off, to
help them in their quest; till her hour came and she sank earthwards
reluctantly, and left them, and mystery once more held field and river.

Then a change began slowly to declare itself. The horizon became
clearer, field and tree came more into sight, and somehow with a
different look; the mystery began to drop away from them. A bird
piped suddenly, and was still; and a light breeze sprang up and set
the reeds and bulrushes rustling. Rat, who was in the stern of the
boat, while Mole sculled, sat up suddenly and listened with a
passionate intentness. Mole, who with gentle strokes was just
keeping the boat moving while he scanned the banks with care,
looked at him with curiosity.

"It's gone!" sighed the Rat, sinking back in his seat again. "So
beautiful and strange and new! Since it was to end so soon, I almost
wish I had never heard it. For it has roused a longing in me that is
pain, and nothing seems worth while but just to hear that sound once
more and go on listening to it for ever. No! There it is again!" he cried,
alert once more. Entranced, he was silent for a long space, spell-
bound.

"Now it passes on and I begin to lose it," he said presently. "Oh

Mole! the beauty of it! The merry bubble and joy, the thin, clear, happy call of the distant piping! Such music I never dreamed of, and the call in it is stronger even than the music is sweet! Row on, Mole, row! For the music and the call must be for us."

The Mole, greatly wondering, obeyed. "I hear nothing myself," he said, "but the wind playing in the reeds and rushes and osiers."

The Rat never answered, if indeed he heard. Rapt, transported, trembling, he was possessed in all his senses by this new divine thing that caught up his helpless soul and swung and dandled it, a powerless but happy infant, in a strong sustaining grasp.

In silence Mole rowed steadily, and soon they came to a point where the river divided, a long backwater branching off to one side. With a slight movement of his head Rat, who had long dropped the rudder-lines, directed the rower to take the backwater. The creeping tide of light gained and gained, and now they could see the colour of the flowers that gemmed the water's edge.

"Clearer and nearer still," cried the Rat joyously. "Now you must surely hear it! Ah—at last—I see you do!"

Breathless and transfixed the Mole stopped rowing as the liquid run of that glad piping broke on him like a wave, caught him up, and possessed him utterly. He saw the tears on his comrade's cheeks, and bowed his head and understood. For a space they hung there, brushed by the purple loosestrife that fringed the bank; then the clear imperious summons that marched hand-in-hand with the intoxicating melody imposed its will on Mole, and mechanically he bent to his oaro again. And the light grew steadily stronger, but no birds sang as they were wont to do at the approach of dawn; and but for the heavenly music all was marvellously still.

On either side of them, as they glided onwards, the rich meadow-grass seemed that morning of a freshness and a greenness unsurpassable. Never had they noticed the roses so vivid, the willow-herb so riotous, the meadow-sweet so odorous and pervading. Then the murmur of the approaching weir began to hold the air, and they felt a consciousness that they were nearing the end, whatever it might be, that surely awaited their expedition.

A wide half-circle of foam and glinting lights and shining shoulders of green water, the great weir closed the backwater from bank to bank, troubled all the quiet surface with twirling eddies and floating foam-streaks, and deadened all other sounds with its solemn and soothing rumble. In mid-most of the stream, embraced in the weir's shimmering arm-spread, a small island lay anchored, fringed close with willow and silver birch and alder. Reserved, shy, but full of significance, it hid whatever it might hold behind a veil, keeping it till the hour should come, and, with the hour, those who were called and chosen.

Slowly, but with no doubt or hesitation whatever, and in something of a solemn expectancy, the two animals passed through the broken, tumultuous water and moored their boat at the flowery margin of the island. In silence they landed, and pushed through the blossom and scented herbage and undergrowth that led up to the level ground, till they stood on a little lawn of a marvellous green, set round with Nature's own orchard-trees—crab-apple, wild cherry, and sloe.

"This is the place of my song-dream, the place the music played to me," whispered the Rat, as if in a trance. "Here, in this holy place, here if anywhere, surely we shall find Him!"

Then suddenly the Mole felt a great Awe fall upon him, an awe that turned his muscles to water, bowed his head, and rooted his feet to the ground. It was no panic terror—indeed he felt wonderfully at peace and happy—but it was an awe that smote and held him and, without seeing, he knew it could only mean that some august Presence was very, very near. With difficulty he turned to look for his friend, and saw him at his side cowed, stricken, and trembling violently. And still there was utter silence in the populous bird-haunted branches around them.

Perrine, in Hector Henri Malot's *Nobody's Girl*, would see the rainbow and hear the cuckoo and glory in them. Perrine's cabin, and the dinner she serves her friend, Rosalie, seem especially lovely today, when far too many people seem to value things for their price tags. If you haven't paid a lot for it, then it isn't worth anything.

I couldn't pay, even if I had millions of dollars, for the sunset I am looking at as I write this. There is no store in the world where I can buy a tomato that will have the taste of one picked from my own garden. Like Perrine, I can find roots and berries, edible plants and leaves, in the fields and in the woods. In June, if I take the saucer-sized flower of the elderberry bush, dip it in batter, and cook it like a pancake, its own natural juices will sweeten the batter and it is a delicious, special treat. Our rhubarb patch is, I would guess, a couple of hundred years old, staying the same size year after year, yielding tart, delicious rhubarb for sauce or pie. And then there are the tiny wild strawberries.

What a beautiful planet we live on! I think I appreciate the beauty because I must be in the city so much of the time. But cities could be beautiful too, if we'd care for them, plant more trees and flowers, and never forget people like Perrine, with their capacity for making much out of almost nothing.

Even in the city there is great beauty; the sunset over the Hudson, the sunrise over the East River, gently falling snow covering dirt and ugliness. Sometimes our great cities dull our vision of the city of God, and I know that if I am not able to envision it when I walk through the dirty streets of upper Manhattan, neither will I have a true vision when I am in the loveliness of the countryside. The vision of the city of God is everywhere.

Rosalie was alone in the garden sitting under an apple tree. When she saw Perrine she came to the gate, half pleased, half annoyed.

"I thought that you were not coming any more," she said.

"I've been very busy."

"What with?"

Perrine showed Rosalie her shoes. Then she told her how she had made herself a chemise and the trouble she had had in cutting it.

"Couldn't you borrow a pair of scissors from the people in your house?" asked Rosalie in astonishment.

"There is no one in my house who could lend me scissors," replied Perrine.

"Everybody has scissors!"

Perrine wondered if she ought to keep her abode a secret any longer. She was afraid that if she did so she might offend Rosalie, so she decided to tell her.

"Nobody lives in my house," she said smiling.

"Whatever do you mean?" asked Rosalie with round eyes.

"That's so, and that's why, as I wasn't able to borrow a saucepan to cook my soup in and a spoon to eat it with, I had to make them and I can tell you that it was harder for me to make my spoon than to make my shoes."

"You're joking!"

"No, really."

Then she told her everything, how she had taken possession of the cabin, and made her own cooking utensils, and about her search for eggs, and how she fished and cooked in the gypsy's camping ground.

Rosalie's eyes opened wider still in wonder and delight. She seemed to be listening to a wonderful story.

When Perrine told her how she made her first sorrel soup, she clapped her hands.

"Oh, how delicious! How you must have enjoyed it!" she cried. "What fun!"

"Yes, everything is great fun when things go right," said Perrine; "but when things won't go! I worked three days for my spoon. I couldn't scoop it out properly. I spoiled two large pieces of tin and had only one left. And my! how I banged my fingers with the stones that I had to use in place of a hammer!"

"But your soup, that's what I'm thinking of," said Rosalie.

"Yes, it was good."

"You know," said Perrine, "there's sorrel and carrots, watercress, onions, parsnips, and turnips, and ever so many things to eat that one can find in the fields. They are not quite the same as the cultivated vegetables, but they are good!"

"One ought to know that!"

"It was my father who taught me to know them."

Rosalie was silent for a moment, then she said:

"Would you like me to come and see you?"

"I should love to have you if you'll promise not to tell anyone where I live," said Perrine, delightedly.

"I promise," said Rosalie, solemnly.

"Well, when will you come?"

"On Sunday I am going to see one of my aunts at Saint-Pipoy; on my way back in the afternoon I can stop . . ."

Perrine hesitated for a moment, then she said amiably:

"Do better than just call; stay to dinner with me."

Rosalie, like the real peasant that she was, began to reply vaguely in a ceremonious fashion, neither saying yes nor no; but it was quite plain to see that she wished very much to accept the invitation. Perrine insisted.

"Do come; I shall be so pleased," she said. "I am so lonesome."

"Well, really . . ." began Rosalie.

"Yes, dine with me; that is settled," said Perrine, brightly; "but you must bring your own spoon, because I shall not have the time nor the tin to make another one."

"Shall I bring my bread also? I can . . ."

"I wish you would. I'll wait for you in the gypsies' ground. You'll find me doing my cooking."

Perrine was very pleased at the thought of receiving a guest in her own home . . . there was a menu to compose, provisions to find . . . what an affair! She felt quite important. Who would have said a few days before that she would be able to offer dinner to a friend!

But there was a serious side. Suppose she could not find any eggs or catch a fish! Her menu then would be reduced to sorrel soup only. What a dinner!

But fortune favored her. On Friday evening she found eggs. True, they were only water-hen's eggs, and not so large as the duck's eggs, but then she must not be too particular. And she was just as lucky with her fishing. With a red worm on the end of her line, she managed to catch a fine perch, which was quite sufficient to satisfy her's and Rosalie's appetite. Yet, however, she wanted a dessert, and some gooseberries growing under a weeping willow furnished it. True, they were not quite ripe, but the merit of this fruit is that you can eat it green.

When, late Sunday afternoon, Rosalie arrived at the gypsy camping ground, she found Perrine seated before her fire upon which the soup was boiling.

"I waited for you to mix the yolk of an egg in the soup," said Perrine. "You have only to turn it with your free hand while I gently pour the soup over it; the bread is soaked."

Although Rosalie had dressed herself specially for this dinner, she was not afraid to help. This was play, and it all seemed very amusing to her.

Soon the soup was ready, and it only had to be carried across to the island. This Perrine did.

The cabin door was open, and Rosalie could see before she entered that the place was filled with flowers. In each corner were grouped, in artistic showers, wild roses, yellow iris, cornflowers, and poppies, and the floor was entirely covered with a beautiful soft green moss.

Rosalie's exclamations of delight amply repaid Perrine for all the trouble she had taken.

"How beautiful! Oh, isn't it pretty!" she exclaimed.

On a bed of fresh ferns two large flat leaves were placed opposite each other; these were to serve for plates; and on a very much larger leaf, long and narrow, which is as it should be for a dish, the perch was placed, garnished with a border of watercress. Another leaf, but very small, served as a salt-cellar, also another holding the dessert. Between each dish was a white anemone, its pure whiteness standing out dazzlingly against the fresh verdure.

"If you will sit down . . ." said Perrine, extending her hand. And when they had taken their seats opposite one another the dinner commenced.

Almost everybody has had a special place, a secret place, a magic kingdom. Often we have these special places, when we are children, with a special friend, as Jess and Leslie did.

My special place didn't come to me until long after I was grown up and my children were nearly out of the nest. It's a brook, not a very big brook, and in midsummer it can almost be dry, with pools of water here and there, rather than the busy splashing of early spring when the water is rushing with melting snow. I have several special sitting places by the brook, where I sometimes go to talk with a friend, or where I go to be alone, to meditate, to try to listen for God.

Listening involves inner silence. I cannot listen until all the static is stopped and I am emptied of complaints and requests and questions, empty enough so that I can be filled.

And then, like Jess and Leslie in *Bridge to Terabithia* by Katherine Paterson, I can catch hold of the rope and swing into the kingdom of love.

Jess and Leslie turned and ran up over the empty field behind the old Perkins place and down to the dry creek bed that separated farmland from the woods. There was an old crab apple tree there, just at the bank of the creek bed, from which someone long forgotten had hung a rope.

They took turns swinging across the gully on the rope. It was a glorious autumn day, and if you looked up as you swung, it gave you the feeling of floating. Jess leaned back and drank in the rich, clear color of the sky. He was drifting, drifting like a fat white lazy cloud back and forth across the blue.

"Do you know what we need?" Leslie called to him. Intoxicated as he was with the heavens, he couldn't imagine needing anything on earth.

"We need a place," she said, "just for us. It would be so secret that we would never tell anyone in the whole world about it." Jess came swinging back and dragged his feet to stop. She lowered her voice almost to a whisper. "It might be a whole secret country," she continued, "and you and I would be the rulers of it."

Her words stirred inside of him. He'd like to be a ruler of something. Even something that wasn't real. "OK," he said. "Where could we have it?"

"Over there in the woods where nobody would come and mess it up."

There were parts of the woods that Jess did not like. Dark places where it was almost like being under water, but he didn't say so.

"I know"—she was getting excited—"it could be a magic country like Narnia, and the only way you can get in is by swinging across on this enchanted rope." Her eyes were bright. She grabbed the rope.

"Come on," she said. "Let's find a place to build our castle stronghold."

They had gone only a few yards into the woods beyond the creek bed when Leslie stopped.

"How about right here?" she asked.

"Sure," Jess agreed quickly, relieved that there was no need to plunge deeper into the woods. He would take her there, of course, for he wasn't such a coward that he would mind a little exploring now and then farther in amongst the ever-darkening columns of the tall pines. But as a regular thing, as a permanent place, this was where he would choose to be—here where the dogwood and redbud played hide and seek between the oaks and evergreens, and the sun flung itself in golden streams through the trees to splash warmly at their feet.

"Sure," he repeated himself, nodding vigorously. The underbrush was dry and would be easy to clear away. The ground was almost level. "This'll be a good place to build."

Leslie named their secret land "Terabithia," and she loaned Jess all of her books about Narnia, so he would know how things went in a magic kingdom—how the animals and the trees must be protected and how a ruler must behave. That was the hard part. When Leslie spoke, the words rolling out so regally, you knew she was a proper queen. He could hardly manage English, much less the poetic language of a king.

But he could make stuff. They dragged boards and other materials down from the scrap heap by Miss Bessie's pasture and built their castle stronghold in the place they had found in the woods. Leslie filled a three-pound coffee can with crackers and dried fruit and a one-pound can with strings and nails. They found five old Pepsi bottles which they washed and filled with water, in case, as Leslie said, "of siege."

Like God in the Bible, they looked at what they had made and found it very good.

As the planet grows more crowded, the "hundreds of acres" Mary Ellen Chase describes in *Windswept* are no longer easy to find. Forests are cut down for housing developments, and then a few small trees are planted, trees that will take a generation or more to mature. Suburbia sprawls farther and farther into the countryside. As the population continues to expand, so does the need for housing. And far too often houses are built without love and without excellence, houses that are not expected to stand for hundreds of years, houses that will have no history and little personality.

Once when I was lecturing in a Midwest university, I had a tea break with several of the students. One of them was talking passionately about pollution of water and air, and all the terrible things being done to despoil the planet, while dropping candy papers on the floor.

We need to do less talking and more picking up of candy papers if we are to have respect for the places we live in.

Our family doesn't have the "hundreds of acres" of Windswept, but we do have a house which is over two hundred years old and was built by people of deep faith in God. Building a house used to be a community affair; raising the rooftree itself would take several strong men. Some of the planks in the walls and floors of our house are over two feet wide. The original doors are the "cross and Bible" doors, and the original hardware is all H, "Help Lord," hardware. Men and women have made love in this house, babies have been born, birthdays celebrated, deaths mourned. It is a house full of story, and that, too, was one of the good things we did for our children: let them grow up in a house full of story.

We were in the country on the day of the Bicentennial, and that afternoon we saw a double rainbow stretch across the house to the old trees of the orchard, a double rainbow for the country's double birthday, and these two may never come together again this side of the tomb. But they have come, and we were there.

John Marston first came into possession of Windswept, its hundreds of rough, unkempt acres, its miles of high, rockstrewn coast, its one precipitous headland, cut by the fierce tides into almost a semi-circle within which his house was later to be built, on Advent Sunday in the year 1880. He was fourteen years old at the time. The day, in fact, chanced to be his birthday.

Sixty years then have passed since that day of his sudden, puzzling, even awful inheritance and legacy; yet Advent Sunday has always been so inextricably associated with Windswept that it seems fitting, perhaps even inevitable, that its story should be undertaken on this special November Sunday. Today the snow is deep there and, according to this morning's weather report, the cold intense and bitter. Today the blueberry fields are discernible only as white mounds tumbling steadily downward toward the wooded point three miles eastward from the house; the tips of the alders, leafless and stiff, shudder in the wind; the clumps of dark, ungainly firs and spruces at each corner of the house and on the slope behind the barn, stand black against the snow, their shadows purple in the sunlight. Today the sea is a purplish gray [and] surf foams like thick suds about the treeless islands. . . .

She saw quickly children running in the wind above the sea, their hair blown, their clothes slapping against their brown legs, dogs leaping and barking, and a flock of curlews circling and calling. . . . She summoned before her and as quickly let them go the smell of wild strawberries in the unkempt July grass; the shock of cold water as she raced down white sand into it, afraid of the taunts of the boy who ran with her if she should hesitate; the chugging of lobster fishermen in the early morning, the crazy careening of their boats beside the brightly painted buoys, as they hauled, baited, threw back, and chugged on again; a thousand hours of sun and storm and wind, a thousand fleeting memories merging with one another, a bright tapestry, a magic carpet, woven of the reds and blacks, gold and grays, of returns and welcomes and farewells, of noise and silence, anger and remorse, laughter and resentment, tears swift and painless tears slow and never really quenched. . . .

More swift turning of leaves, more sights and sounds and smells. Blueberries ripening in the sun; ospreys screaming and circling above their nest in the top of a tall, dead pine; the red of cranberries like drops of fresh blood, millions upon millions of drops against the green of their tiny spiralling leaves matting the high, rocky slopes of miles of unfenced land.

The cranberries held her memory longest, longer even than that of her first knowledge of death and its relentless, intruding, sickening grasp. The cranberries, she thought, are red now, ready to be picked and winnowed in the sun and wind.

Praise God from whom all blessings flow;
Praise Him, all creatures here below;
Praise Him above, ye heavenly host:
Praise Father, Son, and Holy Ghost.

7

Praise God from Whom
All Blessings Flow

When Meg, Jo, Beth, and Amy gave away their Christmas breakfast, they weren't thinking of merit badges or getting credit. It was a spontaneous gesture of generosity to people less fortunate than they were.

Two things came to me as I reread this story. The first was that we get far more pleasure out of giving spontaneously than when we're giving in order to get praise or credit. When we're looking for approval, we tend to want more approval than anyone else, and that becomes more important than the giving. In fact, we are giving to get, rather than to give. Once more we are like the Pharisee, puffed up with pride, rather than the widow giving her mite.

The other thing that came clear to me was that the March girls gave to a particular family, people with names, people whose stories they could share. And while it may not be easy today for us to take our breakfast to our less fortunate neighbors, we do have many ways in which we can give. I have a number of friends who display photographs of their "adopted" children all over the world, children they may never see in person, but whom they are helping to support.

Time is something else we can give, something very valuable. To take time to put down whatever you are doing and listen to someone who needs to talk is a way open to all of us of offering nourishment. Usually the listening ear is what is needed, rather than advice. We are a generous people, we Americans. Whenever there is a plea on television for a needy community or a needy child, we dig deep into our pockets or our checkbooks to help out. So, as we give, whether it's money, or time, or prayer, we too "give up our breakfasts and eat dry bread and drink water" and sing "Praise God from whom all blessings flow."

No one believed in this generosity more than Louisa May Alcott, writing in *Little Women:*

"Merry Christmas, Marmee! Many of them! Thank you for our books; we read some, and mean to every day," they cried, in chorus.

"Merry Christmas, little daughters! I'm glad you began at once, and hope you will keep on. But I want to say one word before we sit down. Not far away from here lies a poor woman with a little new-born baby. Six children are huddled into one bed to keep from freezing, for they have no fire. There is nothing to eat over there; and the oldest boy came to tell me they were suffering hunger and cold. My girls, will you give them your breakfast as a Christmas present?"

They were all unusually hungry, having waited nearly an hour, and for a minute no one spoke; only a minute, for Jo exclaimed impetuously,—

"I'm so glad you came before we began!"

"May I go and help carry the things to the poor little children?" asked Beth eagerly.

"*I* shall take the cream and the muffins," added Amy, heroically giving up the articles she most liked.

Meg was already covering the buckwheats, and piling the bread into one big plate.

"I thought you'd do it," said Mrs. March, smiling as if satisfied. "You shall all go and help me, and when we come back we will have bread and milk for breakfast, and make it up at dinner-time."

They were soon ready, and the procession set out. Fortunately it was early, and they went through back streets, so few people saw them, and no one laughed at the queer party.

A poor, bare, miserable room it was, with broken windows, no fire, ragged bed-clothes, a sick mother, wailing baby, and a group of pale, hungry children cuddled under one old quilt, trying to keep warm.

How the big eyes stared and the blue lips smiled as the girls went in!

"Ach, mein Gott! it is good angels come to us!" said the poor woman, crying for joy.

"Funny angels in hoods and mittens," said Jo, and set them laughing.

In a few minutes it really did seem as if kind spirits had been at work there. Hannah, who had carried wood, made a fire, and stopped up the broken panes with old hats and her own cloak. Mrs. March gave the mother tea and gruel, and comforted her with promises of help, while she dressed the little baby as tenderly as if it had been her own. The girls, meantime, spread the table, set the children round the fire, and fed them like so many hungry birds,— laughing, talking, and trying to understand the funny broken English.

"Das ist gut!" "Die Engel-kinder!" cried the poor things, as they ate, and warmed their purple hands at the comfortable blaze.

The girls had never been called angel children before, and thought it very agreeable, especially Jo, who had been considered a "Sancho" ever since she was born. That was a very happy breakfast, though they didn't get any of it; and when they went away, leaving comfort behind, I think there were not in all the city four merrier people than the hungry little girls who gave away their breakfasts and contented themselves with bread and milk on Christmas morning.

Often it takes some kind of calamitous event for us to recognize the uniqueness of those closest to us. We take each other for granted. We don't listen. We lose great chunks of time and people by not recognizing the terrible uniqueness of every moment and every person in our lives.

This sudden awareness is movingly described by Hugh Walpole in *Jeremy*. It wasn't until Jeremy's mother became very ill, and it looked as though she might die, that he really *recognized* her. And so it is with all of us. We lose that sense of wonder about each other as we lose it about God and all of creation. Little things. Wondrous things. When my grandmother got new sheets or towels, she embroidered her name on them, in red, and the date. Why is that wondrous? I'm not sure, but it is, and I still thrill when I see a sheet with the red embroidery and the date of a year long before I was born.

My grandfather was ambidextrous and wrote with whichever hand was nearer the pen, and that was a wonder too. My mother had beautiful wavy hair, with a wide forehead and a deep widow's peak, and she never knew she was beautiful. My father, during World War I, before I was born, was called Bonnie Prince Charlie by his men and had a volatile temper and an immediate response to all beauty.

In reading about Jeremy's sudden anguished awareness of his mother, my own awareness is reawakened, for my mother, my husband, my children . . . and for the God who is the Maker of us all, and who will never abandon any part of creation.

"Very quietly, children. . . . Your mother—" She broke off as though she were afraid of showing emotion.

"What is it?" said Jeremy in a voice that seemed new to them all—older, more resolute, strangely challenging for so small a boy.

"Your mother's very ill, Jeremy, dear."

. . . He sat on his favourite seat on the window-ledge, dragged up a reluctant Hamlet to sit with him, and gazed out down into the garden that was misty now in the evening golden light, the trees and the soil black beneath the gold, the rooks slowly swinging across the sky above the farther side of the road. Hamlet wriggled. . . . Jeremy held his neck in a vice, and dug his fingers well into the skin. Hamlet whined, then lay still. . . .

Jeremy sat there whilst the dusk fell and all the beautiful lights were drawn from the sky and the rooks went to bed. . . . [He then] dragged out his toy village and pretended to play with it. He looked at his sisters. They seemed quite tranquil. Helen was sewing, and Mary deep in "The Pillars of the House." The clock ticked. Hamlet, lost in sleep, snored and sputtered; the whole world pursued its ordinary way. Only in himself something was changed; he was unhappy, and he could not account for his unhappiness. It should have been because his mother was ill, and yet she had been ill before, and he had been only disturbed for a moment. After all, grown-up people always got well. There had been Aunt Amy, who had had measles, and the wife of the Dean, who had had something, and even the Bishop once. . . . But now he was frightened. There was some perception, coming to him now for the first time in his life, that this world was not absolutely stable—that people left it, people came into it, that there was change and danger and something stronger. . . . Gradually this perception was approaching him as though it had been some dark figure who had entered the house, and now, with muffled step and veiled face, was slowly climbing the stairs towards him. He only knew that his mother could not go; she could not go. She was part of his life, and she would always be so. Why, now, when he thought of it, he could do nothing without his mother; every day he must tell her what he had done and what he was going to do, must show her what he had acquired and must explain to her what he had lost, must go to her when he was hurt and when he was frightened and when he was glad. . . . And of all these things he had never even thought until now.

I can't prove God, and I can't prove heaven, nor that there's a place in it for all who know that God is Love itself and, yes, for me, but I learned long ago that I can't live in a godless world where life has only the most transient meaning, if any. In C. S. Lewis's *The*

Silver Chair, Puddleglum speaks of Aslan and Narnia. Puddleglum was on Aslan's side, whether there was Aslan or not, and he believed in Narnia, whether there was Narnia or not.

I'll go with Puddleglum, just as I'll go with Emily's father's definition of love.

In another book, C. S. Lewis says that one of the cleverest things Satan has done is to make us believe he doesn't exist. Another of Satan's triumphs has been to make far too many people believe that God doesn't exist and that the promises of Love are too good to be true.

They are wonderful promises, yes. They affirm that our lives have meaning; that what God created, God will not abandon; that God loves us far too much to let us be snuffed out at death as though we had never been. They affirm that God has created us to be co-Creators.

But we aren't given false promises. We aren't told that if we get enough merit badges death is not going to come near us, nor illness, nor poverty, nor the horrors of war. We are simply told that we matter, that we matter to God, and that God will be with us, no matter what. And so, no matter what, we can say with Dame Julian of Norwich, "All shall be well and all shall be well and all manner of thing shall be well."

"All you've been saying is quite right, I shouldn't wonder. I'm a chap who always liked to know the worst and then put the best face I can on it. So I won't deny any of what you said. But there's one thing more to be said, even so. Suppose we *have* only dreamed, or made up, all those things—trees and grass and sun and moon and stars and Aslan himself. Suppose we have. Then all I can say is that, in that case, the made-up things seem a good deal more important than the real ones. Suppose this black pit of a kingdom of yours *is* the only world. Well, it strikes me as a pretty poor one. And that's a funny thing, when you come to think of it. We're just babies making up a game, if you're right. But four babies playing a game can make a play-world which licks your real world hollow. That's why I'm going to stand by the play world. I'm on Aslan's side even if there isn't any Aslan to lead it. I'm gong to live as like a Narnian as I can even if there isn't any Narnia. So, thanking you kindly for our supper, if these two gentlemen and the young lady are ready, we're leaving your court at once and setting out in the dark to spend our lives looking for Overland. Nor that our lives will be very long, I should think; but that's small loss if the world's as dull a place as you say."

Growing up in India, the hero of Rudyard Kipling's *Kim* learns many things in his wanderings that most of us do not learn until much later. He learns to revere and care for a very old lama and learns, as a child, how difficult the wearing down of the body can be for the very old.

There is a mystery here that no religion has ever solved in a Q.E.D., "it is proven," kind of way. The spirit of the old lama is far stronger than his body. Physically, the old man leans on Kim. Spiritually, the old man carries him.

It was never more than a couple of miles a day now, and Kim's shoulders bore all the weight of it—the burden of an old man, the burden of the heavy food-bag with the locked books, the load of the writings on his heart, and the details of the daily routine. He begged in the dawn, set blankets for the lama's meditation, held the weary head on his lap through the noonday heats, fanning away the flies till his wrist ached, begged again in the evenings, and rubbed the lama's feet.

"Never was such a *chela*. I doubt at times whether Ananda more faithfully nursed our Lord. And thou art a Sahib? When I was a man—a long time ago—I forgot that. Now I look upon thee often, and every time I remember that thou art a Sahib. It is strange."

"Thou hast said there is neither black nor white. Why plague me with this talk, Holy One? Let me rub the other foot. It vexes me. I am *not* a Sahib. I am thy *chela*, and my head is heavy on my shoulders."

"Patience a little! How far came we to-day in the flesh?"

"Perhaps three-quarters of a mile, and it was a weary march."

"Ha! I went ten thousand thousand in the spirit. How we are all lapped and swathed and swaddled in these senseless things." He looked at his thin blue-veined hand that found the beads so heavy. "*Chela*, hast thou never a wish to leave me?" . . .

"No," he said almost sternly. "I am not a dog or a snake to bite when I have learned to love."

"Thou art too tender for me."

"Not that either. I have moved in one matter without consulting thee. I have sent a message to the Kulu woman saying that thou wast a little feeble and would need a litter. . . . We stay in this place till the litter returns."

"I am content. She is a woman with a heart of gold, as thou sayest, but a talker—something of a talker."

"She will not weary thee. I have looked to that also. Holy One, my heart is very heavy for my many carelessnesses towards thee." A catch rose in his throat. "I have walked thee too far; I have not picked good food always for thee; I have not considered the heat; I have talked to people on the road and left thee alone. . . . I have—I have . . . *Hai mai!* But I love thee . . . and it is all too late. . . . I was a child. . . . Oh, why was I not a man. . . ." Overcome by strain, fatigue, and the weight beyond his years, Kim broke down and sobbed at the lama's feet.

"What a to do is here," said the old man gently. "Thou hast never stepped a hair's breadth from the Way of Obedience. Neglect me? Child—I have lived on thy strength as an old tree lives on the lime of a new wall. Day by day, since Shamlegh Doun, I have stolen strength from thee. *Therefore,* not through any sin of thine, art thou weakened. It is the body—the silly, stupid body—that speaks now. Not the assured soul. Be comforted! . . . We will go to the woman from Kulu. She shall acquire merit in housing us, and specially in tending me. Thou shalt run free till strength returns. I had forgotten the stupid body. If there be any blame, I bear it."

And so he petted and comforted Kim with wise saws and grave texts on that little understood beast, our body, who, being but a delusion, insists on posing as the soul, to the darkening of the Way, and the immense multiplication of unnecessary devils.

"*Hai! hai!* Let us talk of the woman from Kulu. Think you she will ask another charm for her grandsons? When I was a young man, a very long time ago, I was plagued with these vapours, and some others, and I went to an abbot—a very holy man and a seeker after truth, though then I knew it not. Sit up and listen, child of my soul! My tale was told. Said he to me, '*Chela,* know this. There are many lies in the world, and not a few liars, but there are no liars like our bodies' . . . Considering this I was comforted, and of his great favour he suffered me to drink tea in his presence. Suffer me now to drink tea, for I am thirsty."

With a laugh above his tears, Kim kissed the lama's feet, and went about tea-making.

"Thou leanest on me in the body, Holy One, but I lean on thee for all other things. Dost thou know it?"

"I have guessed maybe," and the lama's eyes twinkled.

In my book *A Circle of Quiet* I wonder how much we should protect our children.

I'm like most mothers; my immediate instinct is protective. I tend to be very much a mother lion when it comes to my cubs. But then I remember the eagles, who also love their fledglings. The story goes that in their great, beautiful nests, protected from all danger by their tremendous height, where no marauder can menace the little ones, the mother and father eagle carefully weave thorns. Those thorns are sharply turned inwards so that the fledglings won't be *too* comfortable. . . .

An example of the permanent effect of a book is that of E. B. White's *Charlotte's Web* on our elder daughter. She read it at the age of eight, and when she had finished she was in a mood all day very close to tears because of Charlotte's death at the end. I tried to explain to her that, according to the spider calendar, Charlotte had lived to be a very old lady and had had a fine life. She had lived as long as any spider does, and longer than many. But that only partially comforted her. Then we came to Wilbur the pig.

"Mother," she said, "why did Mr. Zuckerman want to kill Wilbur?"

"Well, Mr. Zuckerman was a farmer, and farmers do kill pigs and sell them for meat."

"Have *we* ever eaten pig?"

"Yes. Often."

"When?"

"Well, whenever we have ham, that's pig. Or bacon. Or pork chops. Or sausage."

"I *hate* sausage!"

Sausage had always been one of her favorite dishes. . . . The entire conversation above is reproduced, verbatim, from my journal.

Wilbur the pig left his mark, whether she remembers it or not. But has it blighted her life? . . . Do we want unmarked children? Are they to go out into the adult world all bland and similar and unscarred? Is wrapping in cotton wool, literary or otherwise, the kind of guidance we owe them?

There's much to be learned from Wilbur and Charlotte, the inevitability of death, the indubitable fact that all life lives in one way or another at the expense of other life, and that life itself is a gift even more extraordinary than rainbows and the song of the cuckoo.

All winter Wilbur watched over Charlotte's egg sac as though he were guarding his own children. He had scooped out a special place in the manure for the sac, next to the board fence. On very cold nights he lay so that his breath would warm it. For Wilbur, nothing in life was so important as this small round object—nothing else mattered. Patiently he awaited the end of winter and the coming of the little spiders. Life is always a rich and steady time when you are waiting for something to happen or to hatch. The winter ended at last.

"I heard the frogs today," said the old sheep one evening. "Listen! You can hear them now."

Wilbur stood still and cocked his ears. From the pond, in shrill chorus, came the voices of hundreds of little frogs.

"Springtime," said the old sheep, thoughtfully. "Another spring." As she walked away, Wilbur saw a new lamb following her. It was only a few hours old. . . . One fine sunny morning, after breakfast, Wilbur stood watching his precious sac. He wasn't thinking of anything much. As he stood there, he noticed something move. He stepped closer and stared. A tiny spider crawled from the sac. It was no bigger than a grain of sand, no bigger than the head of a pin. Its body was grey with a black stripe underneath. Its legs were grey and tan. It looked just like Charlotte.

Wilbur trembled all over when he saw it. The little spider waved at him. Then Wilbur looked more closely. Two more little spiders crawled out and waved. They climbed round and round on the sac, exploring their new world. Then three more little spiders. Then eight. Then ten. Charlotte's children were here at last.

Wilbur's heart pounded. He began to squeal. Then he raced in circles, kicking manure into the air. Then he turned a back flip. Then he planted his front feet and came to stop in front of Charlotte's children.

"Hello, there!" he said.

The first spider said hello, but its voice was so small Wilbur couldn't hear it.

"I am an old friend of your mother's," said Wilbur. "I'm glad to see you. Are you all right? Is everything all right?"

The little spiders waved their forelegs at him. Wilbur could see by the way they acted that they were glad to see him.

"Is there anything I can get you? Is there anything you need?"

The young spiders just waved. For several days and several nights they crawled here and there, up and down, around and about, waving at Wilbur, trailing tiny draglines behind them, and exploring their home. There were dozens and dozens of them. . . .

Then came a quiet morning when Mr. Zuckerman opened a door on the north side. A warm draft of rising air blew softly through the barn cellar. The air smelled of the damp earth, of the spruce woods, of the sweet springtime. The baby spiders felt the warm updraft. One spider climbed to the top of the fence. Then it did something that came as a great surprise to Wilbur. The spider stood on its head, pointed its spinnerets in the air, and let loose a cloud of fine silk. The silk formed a balloon. As Wilbur watched, the spider let go of the fence and rose into the air.

"Good-bye!" it said, as it sailed through the doorway.

"Wait a minute!" screamed Wilbur. "Where do you think you're going?"

But the spider was already out of sight. Then another baby spider crawled to the top of the fence, stood on its head, made a balloon, and sailed away. Then another spider. Then another. The air was soon filled with tiny balloons, each balloon carrying a spider.

Wilbur was frantic. Charlotte's babies were disappearing at a great rate.

"Come back, children!" he cried.

"Good-bye!" they called. "Good-bye, good-bye!"

At last one little spider took time enough to stop and talk to Wilbur before making its balloon.

"We're leaving here on the warm updraft. This is our moment for setting forth. We are aeronauts and we are going out into the world to make webs for ourselves."

"But *where?*" said Wilbur.

"Wherever the wind takes us. High, low. Near, far. East, west. North, south. We take to the breeze, we go as we please."

"Are *all* of you going?" asked Wilbur. "You can't *all* go. I would be left alone, with no friends. Your mother wouldn't want that to happen, I'm sure."

The air was now so full of balloonists that the barn cellar looked almost as though a mist had gathered. Balloons by the dozen were rising, circling, and drifting away through the door, sailing off on the gentle wind. Cries of "Good-bye, good-bye, good-bye!" came weakly to Wilbur's ears. He couldn't bear to watch any more. In sorrow he sank to the ground and closed his eyes. This seemed like the end of the world, to be deserted by Charlotte's children. Wilbur cried himself to sleep.

When he woke it was late afternoon. He looked at the egg sac. It was empty. He looked into the air. The balloonists were gone. Then he walked drearily to the doorway, where Charlotte's web used to be. He was standing there, thinking of her, when he heard a small voice.

"Salutations!" it said. "I'm up here."

"So am I," said another tiny voice.

"So am I," said a third voice. "Three of us are staying. We like this place, and we like *you.*"

Wilbur looked up. At the top of the doorway three small webs were being constructed. On each web, working busily, was one of Charlotte's daughters.

"Can I take this to mean," asked Wilbur, "that you have definitely decided to live here in the barn cellar, and that I am going to have *three* friends?"

"You can indeed," said the spiders.

"What are your names, please?" asked Wilbur, trembling with joy.

Abel and Amanda in William Steig's *Abel's Island* have the kind of love that cannot be separated by time and space. Their love was *love*, rather than a relationship. The word *"relationship"* didn't become jargon until recently. Before that we had friendship, and we had love. Now we have relationships, and many people think that a relationship is not fulfilled unless it ends in bed, whether there's love there or not. One can have a relationship without deep and permanent commitment. But real friendship, like real love, cannot exist without commitment.

"Love is not love which alters when it alteration finds," writes Shakespeare. Love is not love when it does not continue during absence and after death. Abel and Amanda did not have to be present to each other in the flesh to love each other. And they were able to *kythe*.

Kythe is a word I found in an ancient Scottish dictionary of my grandfather's, and it means to communicate with someone with love, beyond barriers of time and space. It is far more than ordinary ESP, which does not necessarily include love. Kything cannot happen without love.

One of the prayers in the Episcopal Church talks of the great cloud of witnesses by whom we are surrounded, those who have died before us and from whom, because of God and his love for us in Christ, we can never be totally separated.

Abel did not know whether or not Amanda was alive or dead, or whether he would ever see her again. But he kythed with Amanda.

By the end of the month of August he knew he was an inhabitant of the island, whether he liked it or not. It was where he lived, just as a prison is where a prisoner lives. He thought constantly of Amanda. He thought of his parents, his brothers, sisters, friends. He knew they were grieving and he was moved by their grief. He, at least, knew he was alive. They didn't. What was Amanda doing? How did her days drag out? Did she still write poetry? Was she able to eat, to sleep, to enjoy her existence in any way? . . .

Wherever he went about the island, he wore Amanda's scarf around his neck, the ends tied in a knot. He would not leave it in the log.

It was September when Abel evolved another scheme for getting home. He would catapult himself across the stream. With his clothes stuffed full of grass for a cushioned landing, using a small stump as a winch, he tried with a rope to bend a sapling down to the ground so it could fling him over the water. But he managed to bend it only two and half tails. That was all the wood yielded to his strength. So this scheme, too, miscarried.

A few days later he succeeded in making fire. He had learned about the primitive methods in school, but he had never tried for himself. After a series of failures, he finally found the right kind of stick to twirl in the right piece of dry wood, and the right kind of tinder to flare with the first flame. His fires were as magical to him as they had been to his prehistoric ancestors.

He first used his fires for smoke beacons, to attract the attention of some civilized being who might just possibly be among the trees on the far shores. When he had a fire burning, he would partially cover it with damp leaves so that it sent up a thick white smoke.

He learned to roast his seeds by placing them on rocks close to the fire. Later he was able to cook various vegetables, flavored with wild garlic or onions, in pots made of a reddish clay from the lower end of the island. The clay was baked hard in prolonged, intense firing.

He also made paper-thin bowls of this clay, and from time to time he would float one down the river with a note in it, and a flower or sprig of grass sticking out to attract notice. One of his notes:

Whoever finds this: Please forward it to my wife, Amanda di Chirico Flint, 89 Bank Street, Mossville.

DEAREST ANGEL—I am ALIVE! I am alone on an island, marooned, somewhere above where this note will be found, God willing. There is a tall cherry birch on the northern end of the island. The island is about 12,000 tails long and is below a waterfall. Do not worry, but send help.

> My utmost and entire love,
> ABEL

Whoever finds this, please send help too. I will be able to give a substantial reward. . . .

During the equinoctial rains, he spent the whole of a dismal day indoors, listening to the unceasing downpour on the outside of his log, watching it through his door and through portholes he had made—the infinite pall of falling rain, the sagging, wet vegetation, the drops dripping from everything as if counting themselves, the runnels and pools, the misty distances—and feeling an ancient melancholy.

Rain caused one to reflect on the shadowed, more poignant parts of life—the inescapable sorrows, the speechless longings, the disappointments, the regrets, the cold miseries. It also allowed one the leisure to ponder questions unasked in the bustle of brighter days; and if one were snug under a sound roof, as Abel was, one felt somehow mothered, though mothers were nowhere around, and absolved of responsibilities. Abel had to cherish his dry log.

At night, when it cleared up, he went out in the wet grass and watched a young moon vanishing behind clouds and reappearing, over and over, like a swimmer out on the sea. Then he went inside the log, barred the entrance, and lay down with Amanda's scarf. . . .

The feeling that he could visit Amanda in dreams haunted Abel. Perhaps he could reach her during his waking hours as well. He began sending her "mind messages." Sitting in the crotch of his favorite branch on the birch, he would project his thoughts, feelings, questions, yearnings, in what he considered the direction of his home. Sometimes he felt that Amanda could "hear" these messages and was responding with loving messages of her own. This feeling elated him.

He became convinced he could fly to his wife through the air, or glide, like a flying squirrel. He made a glider by stretching a catalpa leaf across two sticks, attached it to his back, and climbed to the top of his birch. From there he flung himself into the void, arms outstretched, aiming for the far shore. Instead of the soaring ride he had anticipated, he made a slow, graceful half circle, heels over head, and thudded down on his back in the grass. He lay there for several hours, brokenhearted and dazed with pain.

When body and spirits recovered, he took to climbing his birch again. One day, when he was winding his way upward, around and around the trunk, it seemed to him that the tree was somehow aware of his ascending spiral, and that it enjoyed his delicate scurryings, just as he enjoyed the rugged toughness and sensible architecture of the tree. He felt the tree knew his feelings, though no words could pass between them.

He believed in his "visits" with Amanda; he had his birch, and his star, and the conviction grew in him that the earth and the sky knew he was there and also felt friendly; so he was not really alone, and not really entirely lonely.

The Secret Garden by Frances Hodgson Burnett is the garden of the heart as well as the walled English garden Mary Lennox discovers. Mary comes to Yorkshire as spoiled and nasty and self-centered a child as we can imagine, and her journey into love for others is the journey into the secret garden. Her lessons come not only from Ben Weatherstaff, the old gardener, and Dickon, the Yorkshire boy, but also from Colin, who is as spoiled as she is.

It was shocking to me to learn that *The Secret Garden* had been put on a burn-the-book list because Dickon uses magic. But magic, as expressed by Dickon, is part of the love of God, that love which brings out that which is best for the creature.

Colin had never been to church or been taught anything about God's love, so it was natural for him, too, to use the word "Magic" for the Work of God.

The result of the "Magic" that cured Colin, not only of his physical ailments but also of the tantrums of a spoiled and self-centered boy, was praise, praise of the God who is Love itself.

"What are you thinking about, Ben Weatherstaff?" he asked.

"I was thinkin'," answered Ben, "as I'd warrant tha's gone up three or four pound this week. I was lookin' at tha' calves an' tha' shoulders. I'd like to get thee on a pair o' scales."

"It's the Magic and—and Mrs. Sowerby's buns and milk and things," said Colin. "You see the scientific experiment has succeeded."

That morning Dickon was too late to hear the lecture. When he came he was ruddy with running and his funny face looked more twinkling than usual. As they had a good deal of weeding to do after the rains they fell to work. They always had plenty to do after a warm deep sinking rain. The moisture which was good for the flowers was also good for the weeds which thrust up tiny blades of grass and points of leaves which must be pulled up before their roots took too firm hold. Colin was as good at weeding as any one in these days and he could lecture while he was doing it.

"The Magic works best when you work yourself," he said this morning. "You can feel it in your bones and muscles. I am going to read books about bones and muscles, but I am going to write a book about Magic. I am making it up now. I keep finding out things."

It was not very long after he had said this that he laid down his trowel and stood up on his feet. He had been silent for several minutes and they had seen that he was thinking out lectures, as he often did. When he dropped his trowel and stood upright it seemed to Mary and Dickon as if a sudden strong thought had made him do it. He stretched himself out to his tallest height and he threw out his arms exultantly. Color glowed in his face and his strange eyes widened with joyfulness. All at once he had realized something to the full.

"Mary! Dickon!" he cried. "Just look at me!"

They stopped their weeding and looked at him.

"Do you remember that first morning you brought me in here?" he demanded.

Dickon was looking at him very hard. . . .

"Aye, that we do," he answered.

Mary looked hard too, but she said nothing.

"Just this minute," said Colin, "all at once I remembered it myself—when I looked at my hand digging with the trowel—and I had to stand up on my feet to see if it was real. And it *is* real! I'm *well*—I'm *well!*"

"Aye, that tha' art!" said Dickon.

"I'm well! I'm well!" said Colin again, and his face went quite red all over.

He had known it before in a way, he had hoped it and felt it and thought about it, but just at that minute something had rushed all through him—a sort of rapturous belief and realization and it had been so strong that he could not help calling out.

"I shall live forever and ever and ever!" he cried grandly. "I shall find out thousands and thousands of things. I shall find out about people and creatures and everything that grows—like Dickon—and I shall never stop making Magic. I'm well! I'm well! I feel—I feel as if I want to shout out something—something thankful, joyful!"

Ben Weatherstaff, who had been working near a rose-bush, glanced around at him.

"Tha' might sing th' Doxology," he suggested in his dryest grunt. He had no opinion of the Doxology and he did not make the suggestion with any particular reverence.

But Colin was of an exploring mind and he knew nothing about the Doxology.

"What is that?" he inquired.

"Dickon can sing it for thee, I'll warrant," replied Ben Weatherstaff.

Dickon answered with his all-perceiving animal charmer's smile.

"They sing it i' church," he said. "Mother says she believes th' skylarks sings it when they gets up i' th' mornin'."

"If she says that, it must be a nice song," Colin answered. "I've never been in a church myself. I was always too ill. Sing it, Dickon. I want to hear it."

Dickon was quite simple and unaffected about it. He understood what Colin felt better than Colin did himself. He understood by a sort of instinct so natural that he did not know it was understanding. He pulled off his cap and looked round still smiling.

"Tha' must take off tha' cap," he said to Colin, "an' so mun tha', Ben—an' tha' mun stand up, tha' knows."

Colin took off his cap and the sun shone on and warmed his thick hair as he watched Dickon intently. Ben Weatherstaff scrambled up from his knees and bared his head too with a sort of puzzled half-resentful look on his old face as if he didn't know exactly why he was doing this remarkable thing.

Dickon stood out among the trees and rosebushes and began to sing in quite a simple matter-of-fact way and in a nice strong boy voice:

> "Praise God from whom all blessings flow,
> Praise Him all creatures here below,
> Praise Him above, ye Heavenly Host,
> Praise Father, Son, and Holy Ghost.
>
> Amen."

When he had finished, Ben Weatherstaff was standing quite still with his jaws set obstinately but with a disturbed look in his eyes fixed on Colin. Colin's face was thoughtful and appreciative.

"It is a very nice song," he said. "I like it. Perhaps it means just what I mean when I want to shout out that I am thankful to the Magic." He stopped and thought in a puzzled way. "Perhaps they are both the same thing. How can we know the exact names of everything? Sing it again, Dickon. Let us try, Mary. I want to sing it, too. It's my song. How does it begin? 'Prase God from whom all blessings flow'?"

And they sang it again, and Mary and Colin lifted their voices as musically as they could and Dickon's swelled quite loud and beautiful—and at the second line Ben Weatherstaff raspingly cleared his throat and at the third he joined in with such vigor that it seemed almost savage and when the "Amen" came to an end Mary observed that the very same thing had happened to him which had happened when he found out that Colin was not a cripple—his chin was twitching and he was staring and winking and his leathery old cheeks were wet.

"I never seed no sense in th' Doxology afore," he said hoarsely, "but I may change my mind i' time."

In a letter I received recently, a child asked me, "How can I stay a child forever and never grow up?"

And I replied, "I don't think you can, and I don't think it would be a good idea if you could. What you can do, and what I hope you will do, is stay a child forever and grow up."

In different words, Jesus said that unless we become as little children, we cannot enter the Kingdom of Heaven. And he thanked the Father that these things have been hidden from those who are wise only in the ways of this world and have been revealed to children.

Only as I keep in touch with the child within my very grown-up body can I keep open enough to recognize the God who is Love itself, as that Love is revealed in story. Jesus was a great storyteller, and some of his stories are sad, and some of his stories are scary, and some are funny. I can't read the story of the nasty judge and the importunate widow without laughing.

Of course, if we had been able to include in this anthology all the stories we wanted, it would have run to many volumes. But these few stories will have to stand as examples, and if they do no more than remind us that we can't help loving God, for God is Love itself, then that will be enough.

> There was a time when meadow, grove, and stream,
> The earth, and every common sight,
> To me did seem
> Apparell'd in celestial light.

For Wordsworth, as for most of us,

> The things which I have seen I now can see no more.

The stories in this anthology are reminders of that celestial light, and that "trailing clouds of glory do we come from God, who is our home."

Index of Authors
and Titles

Boldface page numbers indicate excerpts.

Index
of Characters